Block Scheduling:
Implications for
Music Education

G-5356
$19.95

Block Scheduling: Implications For Music Education

Richard B. Miles

Larry R. Blocher

GIA Publications, Inc.
Chicago

Copyright © 1996
GIA Publications, Inc.
7404 S. Mason Ave.
Chicago, IL 60638
1.800.442.1358
www.giamusic.com

Library of Congress Catalog Card Number:
96-61827
ISBN: 0-9655808-0-6

ACKNOWLEDGEMENTS

The authors gratefully acknowledge the many music educators, administrators, students, and colleagues who have shared information concerning the issues addressed in our book. We thank Gail Crum, Information Services Director for the Music Educators National Conference, the office staff of the Morehead State University Bands, especially Ms. Tammy Bradley - former Secretary, and the many undergraduate and graduate students of Morehead State and Wichita State who assisted with the numerous research projects.

We also acknowledge the following for their research grants and funding of the four state surveys on block scheduling:

> The Kentucky Coalition for Music Education
> Kentucky Music Educators Association -
>   District 8
> Indiana Department of Education
> Michigan School Band and Orchestra
>   Association
> Wisconsin Music Educators Association
> Morehead State University, Department of
>   Music and University Bands
> Wichita State University School of Music

Finally, we express gratitude to the many

contributors acknowledged throughout this book who have freely shared information concerning scheduling in their schools.

TABLE OF CONTENTS

Contents

Contents

Contents

INTRODUCTION

Reform - a relatively short word that by itself, looks fairly innocent. When preceded by the word "school", however, the resulting combination, **school reform**, takes on a whole new appearance. A 1994 American Bandmasters Association "Strategic Planning" report, states that " for years we have heard that there are only two things certain in life - death and taxes. We know now that there are three - death, taxes, and school reform." Nationally, at least for now, school reform appears to have become a way of life. And while the "pros" and "cons" of many aspects of school reform will likely continue to be the subject of much informal and formal debate, the realities of the moment seem to dictate the need for information that could be used as a basis for thoughtful decision-making. It has been this perceived need to gather information about block scheduling and school music programs - information that could be used as a basis for informed decision-making - that has been the focus of our research for the past two years.

We were recently asked if we really have a passion for "all that block scheduling stuff." While many words come to mind that would describe the feelings we have had about block scheduling over the past several months, passion is not one of them. We, like many of you, are music teachers. We, like many of you, do have a passion for music and for music teaching. The purpose of this book is to provide information - "stuff" - about block scheduling and school music programs. We simply needed to know more about block scheduling for ourselves, for our colleagues, and for our students. "Truth" is not established. Each reader is challenged to use the material presented here as a starting point for his/her own research and informed decision-making.

CHAPTER 1

Block Scheduling and School Music Programs
- Some Background Information -

Most readers will no doubt be well aquainted with the phrase "alternate use of school time." Additionally, many readers will probably have developed their own "time jargon" vocabulary, or, at the very least, will have heard about or read about the "new" scheduling terminology. Block, double blocked, intensive, pure, modified, full, 4x4, accelerated, split, inbedded, expanded, skinnies, oreo cookie (a personal favorite), zero hour, Copernican Plan... the list seems to grow on a regular basis.

For busy music education professionals, a key question seems to be: "Why should anyone know about or for that matter care about any of these terms?" For music teachers involved as decision-makers in the schools, and for music teachers preparing pre-service music teachers for teaching careers, a "short answer" is because of what these terms involve - a school day divided into larger and generally fewer "blocks" of time per day (those who remember or have read about flexible modular scheduling from three decades ago, may not call the block idea entirely "new"). These "blocks of time", often referred to as "block scheduling", and the many variations on the block scheduling theme that exist, appear to be presenting new challenges for many school music teachers.

Why block scheduling and why now? There may not be one simple answer. Public Law 102-62 (The Education Council Act of 1991) established the National Commission on Time and Learning calling for a "comprehensive review of the relationship between time and learning in the nation's schools." A report prepared by the Commission and released in April of 1994, *Prisoners of Time*, charaterized learning in America's schools as a "prisoner of time" and called for a "reinventing" of schools around learning, not time. At a recent Current Issues in Music Education Symposium held on the campus of the University of Colorado at Boulder, David Berliner, co-author of *The Manufactured Crisis* (1995), stated that "headlines make adults nervous." While "headlines" about scheduling as a part of school reform may be making adults "nervous" leading to action, Robert Canady and Michael Rettig suggest that research may be playing a role in what appears to be a block scheduling movement. In their book, *Block Scheduling: A Catalyst for Change in High Schools* (1995), Canady and Rettig suggest that research conducted in the 1980's involving the traditional, single period schedule, reveals, in part, ineffective use of instruction time within the school day charaterized by time lost to class organization, dealing with student conduct and interruptions, and attending to administrative tasks. Additionally, they suggest that critics of the traditional school schedule describe this type of scheduling as impersonal for students, unfriendly to teachers, and limiting with regard to instructional possibilities - lots of material for headlines and more nervous adults.

On a more positive note, Canady and Rettig state that high school scheduling reform efforts are attempting to reduce the number of class preparations for students and teachers and are encouraging active teaching strategies and student involvement. Block scheduling, when viewed as a part of an educational reform "movement" is an idea whose time has come in many schools. Time will be an important factor in determining success or lack of success in this restructuring effort designed to reinvent schools around learning.

What does this restucturing mean to music teachers? Again, there is probably no simple answer. There is evidence, however, to suggest that block scheduling is an important issue for many music teachers - especially those involved with it now or those gathering information for making decisions about it in the future. The Music Educators National Conference

(MENC) reported requests for information on how to deal with block scheduling from more than 200 schools from 35 states during 1995. The August, 1996 issue of *Teaching Music* identifies block scheduling as the number one reform issue facing public school music teachers. A recent telephone survey conducted in Kansas identified more than 90 Kansas high schools involved with some form of block scheduling during the 1996-97 school year. For music teachers in these schools, block scheduling is a reality. What does that mean?

David Berliner suggests that "education runs on anecdote." Talking about *The Manufactured Crisis*, Berliner, speaking at the Colorado Symposium, stated that "we did something unusual in education - we looked at the data." To a certain extent, the effects of block scheduling on school music programs appears to be running on anecdotal evidence. The empirical evidence that we do have certainly suggests the need for further study. Gary Hall, in his 1992 Masters Thesis, looked at the effects of block scheduling on school music programs in 24 Colorado schools. The results of his study indicated, in part, that enrollments in performing arts classes (band, chorus, orchestra) were decreasing with scheduling problems becoming a major issue for students, especially upper-class students. The 4-period day in Colorado schools was viewed as a major problem for music programs. Results suggested the need for further research.

The Kentucky Department of Education (KDE) in a document entitled **High School Restructuring: Block Scheduling Concerns and Issues**, reported that prior to the 1993-94 school year, no more than a handful of schools in Kentucky were using a block scheduling system. The KDE identified Western High School in Louisville, Kentucky as a pioneer in introducing block scheduling, reporting that many schools had used the "Western" model (at that time) as a basis for their own system. Richard Miles and Loren Waa used information provided by the KDE in November, 1994 to evaluate participation in the music program at Western High School. Results indicated that between the 1990-91 and 1993-94 school years, Western High School experienced a 53% reduction in student participation in high school band and chorus. Scheduling appeared to be a major concern, once again suggesting the need for further study.

For the past two years we have been looking at the impact of block scheduling implementation on performance arts classes - band, chorus, and orchestra. We have looked at nearly 200 school music programs in a 4-state area, asking questions about scheduling types, enrollment trends, and scheduling conflicts. Chapter 2 provides a detailed look "inside" these music

programs.   We have identified high school music
programs from across the country where block
scheduling appears to be working. Chapters 3 and 4
detail this information (sample schedules are included).
The remaining chapters offer suggestions for becoming
involved with and informed about block scheduling. All
of the information included has been provided for music
teachers by music teachers.

CHAPTER 2

A Survey of Block Scheduling Implementation On Secondary School Music Programs in *Kentucky, Indiana, Michigan, and Wisconsin*

Having received many phone calls from our public school colleagues looking for ways to deal with block scheduling, we realized that we had no answers. This is the point at which we became interested in block scheduling. In our search for information, we discovered that while there was no shortage of opinion on block scheduling and school music programs, studies detailing the effects of block scheduling on music performance and non-performance classes were limited and suggested possible negative effects. We decided to look further. After nearly two years of systematically looking for answers, we can say with confidence that we still have no definitive answers. However, we have had the opportunity to look inside school music programs thanks to the efforts of many caring music education professionals. To date, we have gathered information on the effects of block scheduling in four states - Kentucky, Indiana, Michigan, and Wisconsin. An extensive overview of this "look inside" music programs currently using block scheduling follows.

How We Obtained Our Information

We began our look in Kentucky, by sending a questionnaire to all band directors in Kentucky high schools reported by the Kentucky Department of Education to be using some form of block scheduling during the 1994-95 school year. There were 72 schools in all. Each band director was asked to gather information from all secondary music teachers in the school. The questionnaire was designed to gather information about the type of block scheduling currently in use, how long it had been in use, student enrollment information in performance classes (band, chorus, and orchestra) before and after block scheduling implementation, class conflict information, and general school demographic information. A final section of the questionnaire invited open-ended comments from respondents.

While we received responses from 69 of the 72 high schools (96%), we found that four of the schools in Kentucky were not currently using block scheduling. The following outlines the distribution of responding schools by size.

KENTUCKY
22 Small Schools   (001-399 enrollment)
25 Medium Schools (400-799)
<u>18</u> Large Schools   (800+)
65 TOTAL High Schools

We used the same data gathering process in

Indiana, receiving responses from 42 of the 43 schools
(98%) reported by the Indiana Department of
Education to be using some form of block scheduling
during the 1995-96 school year. The 42 responding
schools had the following school size distribution.

INDIANA
 7 Small Schools   (001-399)
19 Medium Schools (400-799)
<u>16</u> Large Schools   (800+)
42 TOTAL Schools

In Michigan, an initial survey of 579 schools
(100% response) identified 61 schools using some form
of block scheduling during the 1995-96 school year. We
received 58 responses from the 61 Michigan schools
(95%). The 58 responding Michigan schools included
the following distribution.

MICHIGAN
19 Small Schools   (001-399)
28 Medium Schools (400-799)
<u>11</u> Large Schools   (800+)
58 TOTAL Schools

The Wisconsin Music Educators Association
identified 34 schools on block scheduling. We again
used the same data gathering process in Wisconsin and
received responses from all 34 schools (100%). We
found that 28 high schools were on block and six were
not currently on block scheduling. The 28 responding
Wisconsin schools had the following school size
distribution.

WISCONSIN
17 Small Schools   (001-399)
 6 Medium Schools (400-799)
 <u>5</u> Large Schools   (800+)
28 TOTAL Schools

Types of Schedules

Our initial questions attempted to determine both the type of block scheduling currently in use in each school, and the length of time each school had been involved with block scheduling. Music teachers in Kentucky schools reported that 60% of their schools were using a full block (4 block day, 4 classes per semester) schedule and 40% were using some form of a modified block. Ninety-four percent of responding Kentucky schools had been involved with block scheduling for at least two years.

In Indiana, music teachers indicated that 23% of their schools were using a full block and 77% were using a modified block. Eighty-three percent of responding Indiana schools had been involved with block scheduling for at least two years.

Michigan music teachers reported that 12% of their schools were using a full block and 88% were using a modified block. All of the responding Michigan schools had been involved with block scheduling for at least two years.

In Wisconsin, responding music teachers reported that 29% of their schools were using a full block schedule and 71% were using some form of a modified block. Eighty-two percent of the responding Wisconsin schools had been involved with block scheduling for at least two years.

The following compares the forms of block scheduling used by small, medium, and large schools in our four state study.

Forms of Block Scheduling

School Size	% FULL Block (4 block day, 4 classes per semester)	% MODIFIED (any form)
KENTUCKY		
Small	59%	41%
Medium	62%	38%
Large	61%	39%
Combined	60%	40%
INDIANA		
Small	43%	57%
Medium	16%	84%
Large	21%	79%
Combined	23%	77%

Forms of Block Scheduling Continued

School Size	% FULL Block (4 block day, 4 classes per semester)	% MODIFIED (any form)
MICHIGAN		
Small	16%	84%
Medium	14%	86%
Large	0%	100%
Combined	12%	88%
WISCONSIN		
Small	29%	71%
Medium	17%	83%
Large	40%	60%
Combined	29%	71%

Please note for future comparisons, that the majority of Kentucky schools reported using the full block form of scheduling. The large majority of Indiana, Michigan, and Wisconsin schools reported using a modified form of scheduling.

In the past two years, few of the schools have changed the form of block scheduling. The following compares the changes by state.

Percentage of Respondent Schools to Change the Form of Block Scheduling in the Past 2 Years

Kentucky   Indiana   Michigan   Wisconsin

From FULL Block to Modified Block

Kentucky	Indiana	Michigan	Wisconsin
5%	2%	2%	11%

From Modified Block to FULL Block

Kentucky	Indiana	Michigan	Wisconsin
6%	4%	2%	14%

Student Enrollment Trends

Music teachers from all four states indicated varying student enrollments in performance classes (band, chorus, and orchestra) since adopting block scheduling. Enrollment trends compared by scheduling type and school size for all schools in each individual state follow.

Enrollment in Performing
Arts Classes

Size/Type	Decreased	Same	Increase

KENTUCKY

Size/Type	Decreased	Same	Increase
Small	53%	33%	14%
Medium	39%	48%	13%
Large	35%	59%	6%
Combined	45%	43%	12%

Comparison by Scheduling Type

	Decreased	Same	Increase
Full Block	44%	46%	1%
Modified	41%	45%	14%

INDIANA

Size/Type	Decreased	Same	Increase
Small	33%	33%	33%
Medium	6%	44%	50%
Large	12%	47%	41%
Combined	14%	43%	43%

Comparison by Scheduling Type

	Decreased	Same	Increase
Full Block	30%	50%	20%
Modified	6%	42%	52%

Enrollment Continued

Size/Type	Decreased	Same	Increase

MICHIGAN

Size/Type	Decreased	Same	Increase
Small	12%	82%	6%
Medium	22%	46%	32%
Large	30%	40%	30%
Combined	22%	54%	24%

Comparison by Scheduling Type

Full Block	43%	57%	0%
Modified	17%	56%	27%

WISCONSIN

Size/Type	Decreased	Same	Increase
Small	29%	53%	18%
Medium	17%	66%	17%
Large	40%	40%	20%
Combined	18%	53%	18%

Comparison by Scheduling Type

Full Block	38%	50%	12%
Modified	25%	55%	20%

When comparing the type of block scheduling and the trend for enrollment in performing arts classes, schools on the full block had a tendency to have a larger percentage of decreased enrollment and a smaller percentage of increased enrollment. In Kentucky where 60% of the respondent schools were on the full block, only one percent of the programs increased enrollment. It is important to recognize that in Indiana, Michigan, and Wisconsin, the large majority of schools used some form of modified scheduling where enrollment increased in at least 20% of the respondent schools (Wisconsin) and in Indiana, 52% of the schools.

Scheduling

Scheduling time for music has been a long-time concern. For decades experimentation with scheduling has included formats similar to block scheduling such as "modular scheduling" incorporated in some schools more than twenty years earlier. Instructional classes have varied from the traditional six period day and have included four to nine classes per day. Grading periods have varied from semester, trimester, to quarter intervals.

Currently, it appears that many schools have moved to another type of alternate scheduling. Some schools have moved to year-round instruction and many have moved to fewer instructional periods per day and fewer grading terms with longer minutes per daily classes. These scheduling changes have brought new scheduling challenges.

Scheduling conflicts have been identified as a primary factor in the reduction of opportunities for some students to continue with a consistent sequential course of study for performance arts classes. If we as educators are to include the most opportunities for our students, we must identify the problems that some have had with block scheduling and attempt to find solutions to these scheduling challenges. Our research has focused on and attempted to identify these scheduling concerns with block scheduling.

The chart that follows helps to clarify some of the conflict potentials that educators face with scheduling time for students to participate in performance arts classes. Please note that the potential conflict with other classes that meet simultaneously for an eight-period day is 12.5% or a ratio of a one-to-eight potential. The conflict with a four-period day is 25% or a ratio of one-to-four. When students must choose 25% of their total class time devoted to music in a single grading period, the potential for conflict has obviously increased. With a student who may participate in band and orchestra, band and chorus, chorus and orchestra, etc., the conflict has increased to a 50% potential. Therefore, the more class choices a student has simultaneously (the eight period form) the greater the potential for the student to enroll with less conflict. The fewer classes available as an option (the four-period day - four classes per semester) the greater the potential conflict.

Scheduling Conflict Potentials

(Ratio and Percentage of Conflict for Each Music Class)

Scheduling System	Ratio of Potential Conflict	Percentage of Potential Conflict
Eight-Period Day	1 to 8	12.5%
Seven-Period Day	1 to 7	14.3%
Six-Period Day	1 to 6	16.7%
Five-Period Day	1 to 5	20%
Four-Period Day	1 to 4	25%

Our research investigated the concerns of music directors with scheduling conflicts which involved Advanced Placement (AP) classes, elective classes, potential conflicts with 11th and 12th grade students, the ability to maintain constant enrollment in ensembles, the ability to maintain balanced instrumentation or balanced vocal parts, the ability to maintain performance proficiency of the performance arts classes, the general success of the performance arts classes, and the ability of students to enroll in more than one music class.

Scheduling Conflicts

In Kentucky, 69% of all music teachers reporting a decrease in student enrollment in performance classes since adopting block scheduling indicated that scheduling conflicts were the primary reason for the decrease.   Forty-five percent of all Indiana music teachers reporting decreased student enrollment indicated that scheduling conflicts were to blame.   In Michigan, 67% of all music teachers reporting a decrease in student enrollment stated that scheduling conflicts were the cause.   Sixty-eight percent of the Wisconsin music teachers reported scheduling conflicts were the reason for decreased participation.   The following outlines the responses by state and school size.

Scheduling Conflicts -
The Primary Reason for
Student Drop Out

School Size   Percentage

KENTUCKY

Small	68%
Medium	71%
Large	72%
Combined	69%

Comparison by Scheduling Type

Full Block	70%
Modified Block	68%

INDIANA

Small	43%
Medium	58%
Large	33%
Combined	45%

Comparison by Scheduling Type

Full Block	50%
Modified Block	44%

MICHIGAN

Small	74%
Medium	64%
Large	64%
Combined	67%

Comparison by Scheduling Type

Full Block	57%
Modified Block	69%

WISCONSIN

Small	81%
Medium	50%
Large	60%
Combined	68%

Comparison by Scheduling Type

Full Block	75%
Modified Block	65%

Advanced Placement Class Conflicts

In Kentucky, 58% of the music teachers reported having conflicts with AP classes causing students to drop out of their performance classes. Twenty-four percent of all Indiana music teachers reported decreased enrollment because of AP conflicts. In

Michigan, 49% indicated AP conflicts and Wisconsin music educators reported that 32% had conflicts with AP classes. The following outlines the responses by state and school size.

Percentage of Schools Where Students Must Drop Out Due to AP Class Conflicts

School Size	Percentage

KENTUCKY

Small	59%
Medium	56%
Large	59%
Combined	58%

Comparison by Scheduling Type

Full Block	58%
Modified Block	56%

INDIANA

Small	0%
Medium	22%
Large	40%
Combined	24%

Comparison by Scheduling Type

Full Block	20%
Modified Block	25%

AP Class Conflicts Continued

School Size	Percentage

MICHIGAN

Small	44%
Medium	48%
Large	55%
Combined	47%

Comparison by Scheduling Type

Full Block	43%
Modified Block	47%

WISCONSIN

Small	24%
Medium	33%
Large	60%
Combined	32%

Comparison by Scheduling Type

Full Block	25%
Modified Block	35%

Elective Class Conflicts

Kentucky music teachers reported that 51% were having scheduling conflicts with other elective classes. Twenty-one percent of Indiana music teachers indicated conflicts with electives, 26% with conflicts in Michigan, and 20% with elective conflicts in Wisconsin. The following represents the distribution of responses by state and school size.

Percentage of Schools Having Scheduling Conflicts With Other Electives

School Size	Percentage
KENTUCKY	
Small	53%
Medium	50%
Large	50%
Combined	51%

Comparison by Scheduling Type

Full Block	55%
Modified Block	48%

Scheduling Conflicts With Other Electives Continued

School Size	Percentage

INDIANA

Small	18%
Medium	22%
Large	27%
Combined	21%

Comparison by Scheduling Type

Full Block	40%
Modified Block	16%

MICHIGAN

Small	29%
Medium	25%
Large	27%
Combined	26%

Comparison by Scheduling Type

Full Block	57%
Modified Block	22%

Scheduling Conflicts With Other
Electives Continued

School Size   Percentage

WISCONSIN

Small	41%
Medium	17%
Large	20%
Combined	20%

Comparison by Scheduling Type

Full Block	13%
Modified Block	40%

Conflicts With Upper Class Students (11-12)

Forty-six percent of all Kentucky music teachers indicated difficulty in keeping upper class students (grades 11-12) enrolled in performance classes since adopting block scheduling. In Indiana, 21% of all music teachers reported difficulty with upper class enrollment, while in Michigan, 43% indicated a similar concern, and 39% in Wisconsin. The following outlines the response percentages by state and school size.

Percentage of Schools
Where Upper Class Students (11-12)
Have Problems Staying Enrolled

School Size   Percentage

KENTUCKY

Small	59%
Medium	51%
Large	33%
Combined	46%

Comparison by Scheduling Type

Full Block	45%
Modified Block	48%

INDIANA

Small	67%
Medium	13%
Large	20%
Combined	21%

Comparison by Scheduling Type

Full Block	30%
Modified Block	19%

Upper Class Students (11-12) Having
Problems Staying Enrolled Continued

School Size   Percentage

MICHIGAN

Small	39%
Medium	48%
Large	45%
Combined	43%

Comparison by Scheduling Type

Full Block	57%
Modified Block	41%

WISCONSIN

Small	24%
Medium	67%
Large	60%
Combined	39%

Comparison by Scheduling Type

Full Block	25%
Modified Block	45%

Balanced Instrumentation and Vocal Parts

When comparing the ability to maintain balanced instrumentation and vocal parts with block scheduling, 23% of the Kentucky music teachers indicated that it was easy to maintain while 50% had difficulty. In Indiana, 33% had an easy time maintaining and 22% found it difficult. Twenty-eight percent of the Michigan music teachers had an easy time maintaining while 33% had difficulty. Only 11% of the Wisconsin music teachers reported maintaining easy while 39% found maintaining difficult.

When comparing the type of block scheduling used in the four states, it is interesting to note that three of the four states reported a higher percentage of difficulty in maintaining balanced instrumentation and vocal parts while using full block scheduling compared to the ability to maintain balance. Under the modified forms of block scheduling, music educators in two states reported it easy to maintain balance with a higher percentage than difficulty and two states indicated more difficulty with a higher percentage compared to being easy to maintain balance. The following outlines the comparison by state, school size, and scheduling type.

Balanced Instrumentation And Vocal Parts With Block Scheduling

Size & Type	Easy to Maintain	No Difference	Difficult to Maintain
KENTUCKY			
Small	35%	15%	50%
Medium	13%	35%	52%
Large	24%	41%	35%
Combined	23%	27%	50%
Comparison by Scheduling Type			
Full Block	22%	32%	46%
Modified	26%	26%	48%
INDIANA			
Small	0%	86%	14%
Medium	61%	22%	17%
Large	21%	64%	14%
Combined	33%	45%	22%
Comparison by Scheduling Type			
Full Block	33%	45%	22%
Modified	37%	50%	13%

Balanced Instrumentation
And Vocal Parts Continued

Size & Type	Easy to Maintain	No Difference	Difficult to Maintain
MICHIGAN			
Small	16%	56%	28%
Medium	29%	41%	30%
Large	40%	30%	30%
Combined	26%	41%	33%
Comparison by Scheduling Type			
Full Block	14%	43%	43%
Modified	29%	44%	27%
WISCONSIN			
Small	12%	53%	35%
Medium	0%	83%	17%
Large	20%	0%	80%
Combined	11%	50%	39%
Comparison by Scheduling Type			
Full Block	0%	50%	50%
Modified	15%	50%	35%

Performance Proficiency

Since adopting block scheduling in Kentucky, 34% of the schools indicated that the performance level of their students had increased. Forty-one percent of the schools reported no difference, and 25% indicated that the overall student performance level had declined. When compared across block schedule type, schools in Kentucky using a full block schedule reported that 47% believed students were performing better, 35% no difference, and 18% indicated a decline in student performance level. For schools using some form of a modified block schedule, 12% reported an increase in student performance level, 50% reported no difference, and 38% indicated a decline in the overall student performance level.

In Indiana, 26% of the schools indicated that the performance level of their students had increased. Forty-three percent of the schools reported no difference, and 31% indicated that the overall student performance level had declined. When compared across block schedule type, schools in Indiana using a full block schedule reported that 22% believed students were performing better, 22% no difference, and 56% indicated a decline in student performance level. For schools using some form of a modified block schedule, 27% reported an increase in student performance level, 50% reported no difference, and 23% indicated a decline in overall student performance level.

Michigan music teachers reported that in 27% of the schools, the performance level of their students had increased. Thirty-nine percent of the schools reported no difference, and 34% indicated that overall student performance level had declined. When compared across block schedule type, schools in Michigan using a full block schedule reported that 57% believed students were performing better, 14% no difference, and 29% indicated a decline in student performance level. For schools using some form of a modified block schedule, 22% reported an increase in student performance level, 43% reported no difference, and 35% indicated a decline in overall student performance level.

Since adopting block scheduling in Wisconsin, 21% of the schools indicated that the performance level of their students had increased. Twenty-five percent of the schools reported no difference, and 54% indicated that overall student performance level had declined. When compared across block schedule type, schools in Wisconsin using a full block schedule reported that 50% believed students were performing better, and 50% indicated a decline in student performance level. For schools using some form of a modified block schedule, 10% reported an increase in student performance level, 35% reported no difference, and 55% indicated a decline in overall student performance level.

The following two pages compares the performance proficiency reported by state, size of school, combined percentage response, and scheduling type.

Performance Proficiency
Of Students on
Block Scheduling

Size & Type	Proficiency Improved	No Difference	Proficiency Declined
KENTUCKY			
Small	23%	45%	32%
Medium	35%	48%	17%
Large	47%	26%	27%
Combined	34%	41%	25%

Comparison by Scheduling Type

Full Block	47%	35%	18%
Modified	12%	50%	38%

Size & Type	Proficiency Improved	No Difference	Proficiency Declined
INDIANA			
Small	57%	29%	14%
Medium	28%	44%	28%
Large	7%	50%	43%
Combined	26%	43%	31%

Comparison by Scheduling Type

Full Block	22%	22%	56%
Modified	27%	50%	23%

Performance Proficiency Continued

Size & Type	Proficiency Improved	No Difference	Proficiency Declined
MICHIGAN			
Small	26%	37%	37%
Medium	33%	44%	22%
Large	10%	30%	60%
Combined	27%	39%	34%

Comparison by Scheduling Type

Full Block	57%	14%	29%
Modified	22%	43%	35%

Size & Type	Proficiency Improved	No Difference	Proficiency Declined
WISCONSIN			
Small	29%	24%	47%
Medium	17%	33%	50%
Large	0%	20%	80%
Combined	21%	25%	54%

Comparison by Scheduling Type

Full Block	50%	0%	50%
Modified	10%	35%	55%

Constant Enrollment

One of the areas which seems to require justification in many schools involves students enrolling in consecutive semesters and consecutive years of performance arts classes. Since classes on the full block scheduling type often complete an entire years credit in one semester, many do not understand the need for sequential year-round instruction in performance arts classes. The following area presents the music teachers responses concerning their ability to maintain constant enrollment while on block scheduling and the percentage of those programs experiencing fluctuating enrollment in performance classes.

Directors in Kentucky reported 57% were able to maintain constant enrollment and 43% had fluctuating enrollment. Those programs on the full block in Kentucky indicated 59% with constant enrollment and 41% had fluctuating enrollment. Schools on a modified block schedule reported 60% with constant enrollment while 40% had fluctuating enrollment.

Indiana directors indicated the 85% of the schools had constant enrollment and 15% had fluctuating enrollment. Sixty-seven percent of the directors using full block scheduling reported constant enrollment and 33% reported enrollment that fluctuated. Modified block schools indicated that 90%

had constant enrollment while only 10% encountered fluctuating enrollment.

In Michigan, music teachers reported 79% with constant enrollment and 21% with fluctuating enrollment. Those programs using the full block reported 57% with constant enrollment and 43% with fluctuating enrollment. Schools on a modified block schedule reported 82% with constant enrollment and 18% had fluctuating enrollment.

Sixty-nine percent of the directors responding in Wisconsin indicated the they were able to maintain constant enrollment and 31% experienced fluctuating enrollment. Wisconsin programs using the full block reported 63% with constant enrollment and 37% with fluctuating enrollment. Programs using modified scheduling forms were reported to have 72% with constant enrollment while 28% experienced fluctuating enrollment.

The following outlines the comparison of responses by state and scheduling type.

Directors Reporting
Constant Enrollment

School Size	% With Constant Enrollment	% With Fluctuating Enrollment
KENTUCKY		
Small	33%	67%
Medium	48%	52%
Large	59%	41%
Combined	57%	43%
Comparison by Scheduling Type		
Full Block	59%	41%
Modified	60%	40%
INDIANA		
Small	88%	12%
Medium	88%	12%
Large	79%	21%
Combined	85%	15%
Comparison by Scheduling Type		
Full Block	67%	33%
Modified	90%	10%

Constant Enrollment Continued

School Size	% With Constant Enrollment	% With Fluctuating Enrollment

MICHIGAN

Small	82%	18%
Medium	81%	19%
Large	67%	33%
Combined	79%	21%

Comparison by Scheduling Type

Full Block	57%	43%
Modified	82%	18%

WISCONSIN

Small	71%	29%
Medium	100%	0%
Large	25%	75%
Combined	69%	31%

Comparison by Scheduling Type

Full Block	63%	37%
Modified	72%	28%

Enrollment in More Than One
Performance Arts Class

The next area compares the responses of directors with the individual students ability to enroll in more than one performance arts class. Since the adoption of block scheduling, Indiana music teachers reported that it had become more difficult in 44% of the programs but usually no problem in 46% of the programs. When compared across block schedule type, 56% of all Indiana schools using a full block reported increased difficulty while 33% usually had no problem. Those programs on a modified block indicated that 41% had increased difficulty and 50% usually had no problem.

Michigan directors reported that 52% had a problem with students enrolling in more than one performance class while 32% usually had no problem. Schools on the full block schedule were reported to have 57% with problems and 14% usually had no problem. Modified block schools were reported to have 51% with problems and 35% usually with no problems.

Schools in Wisconsin were reported by directors to have 54% with problems enabling students to enroll in one or more performance classes. Thirty-two percent usually had no problem. When compared across block schedule type, 50% of all Wisconsin schools using a full block reported increased difficulty while 38% usually had no problem. Those programs on a modified block indicated that 55% had increased difficulty and 30% usually had no problem.

The following compares enrollment in more than one performance arts class by state, combined response, and scheduling type. *This information was not asked on the Kentucky survey.*

Enrollment in More Than
One Performance Arts Class
(Band, Orchestra, Chorus, Theatre, Dance)

Size & Type	Usually No Problem	No Difference	Yes, A Problem
INDIANA			
Small	37%	25%	38%
Medium	50%	6%	44%
Large	50%	6%	44%
Combined	46%	10%	44%
Comparison by Scheduling Type			
Full Block	33%	11%	56%
Modified	50%	9%	41%

Enrollment in More Than
One Performance Arts Class Continued
(Band, Orchestra, Chorus, Theatre, Dance)

Size & Type	Usually No Problem	No Difference	Yes, A Problem
MICHIGAN			
Small	17%	33%	50%
Medium	41%	7%	52%
Large	36%	9%	55%
Combined	32%	16%	52%

Comparison by Scheduling Type

Full Block	14%	29%	57%
Modified	35%	14%	51%

WISCONSIN			
Small	23%	24%	53%
Medium	67%	0%	33%
Large	20%	0%	80%
Combined	32%	14%	54%

Comparison by Scheduling Type

Full Block	38%	12%	50%
Modified	30%	15%	55%

Block Scheduling and the Success of
Performance Arts Classes

Music teachers were asked to express their opinion of the overall impact of block scheduling on the success of their music programs. Kentucky music teachers reported that block scheduling was a positive factor in 26% of the programs, block scheduling had no impact on their success in 24%, and block scheduling was a negative factor in 50% of the programs.

Indiana music teachers indicated block scheduling was a positive factor in 51% of the programs, made no difference in 28%, and was a negative factor in 21% of the programs.

In Michigan, 34% of the music teachers reported block scheduling being a positive factor, 22% experienced no difference, while 44% reported block scheduling being a negative factor.

Twenty-five percent of Wisconsin music teachers indicated block scheduling was a positive factor, 21% no difference, and 54% reported that block scheduling was a negative factor.

The following outlines the responses by state, size of school, combined response, and scheduling type.

Block Scheduling
And the Success of
Performance Arts Classes

Size & Type	Positive Factor	No Difference	Negative Factor
KENTUCKY			
Small	19%	19%	62%
Medium	21%	37%	42%
Large	41%	12%	47%
Combined	26%	24%	50%

Comparison by Scheduling Type

Full Block	26%	29%	45%
Modified	25%	17%	58%

Size & Type	Positive Factor	No Difference	Negative Factor
INDIANA			
Small	72%	14%	14%
Medium	39%	39%	22%
Large	53%	27%	20%
Combined	51%	28%	21%

Comparison by Scheduling Type

Full Block	44%	12%	44%
Modified	53%	33%	14%

The Success of
Performance Arts Classes Continued

Size & Type	Positive Factor	No Difference	Negative Factor
MICHIGAN			
Small	24%	29%	47%
Medium	41%	22%	37%
Large	40%	0%	60%
Combined	34%	22%	44%

Comparison by Scheduling Type

Full Block	43%	14%	43%
Modified	33%	23%	44%

Size & Type	Positive Factor	No Difference	Negative Factor
WISCONSIN			
Small	29%	24%	47%
Medium	17%	33%	50%
Large	20%	0%	80%
Combined	25%	21%	54%

Comparison by Scheduling Type

Full Block	50%	0%	50%
Modified	15%	30%	55%

Administration Views

Research by Greenwood (1991)[1] and Greenwood and Dunnigan (1993)[2] suggested one of the major factors in the success of school music programs was the direct influence and intervention of the school administration. In our study, music teachers were asked to report their opinion of their administrators view concerning participation in performance arts classes and if the administrators viewed performance arts classes as an important part of the students' overall education. The following outlines the responses by state (see the next page). It is important to note that in each state, the majority of administrators appear to value performance arts classes. This may be an essential element in the development of a positive working relationship to resolve scheduling challenges and conflicts.

---

[1] Greenwood, R. A. (1991). Secondary school administrators' attitudes and perceptions on the role of music and school bands. Doctoral dissertation, The Florida State University.

[2] Greenwood, R. A. (1993, February). Secondary school principals' opinions on the relationship between budget and various school curricula. Report and paper presented at the 27th National Convention of the College Band Directors National Association, The Ohio State University, Columbus, Ohio.

Administration Views
Participation in Performance Arts Classes
As an Important Part of
The Students' Overall Education

	Important	Not Important
KENTUCKY	53%	47%
INDIANA	57%	43%
MICHIGAN	57%	43%
WISCONSIN	64%	36%

Music Teacher Comments

The final section of the questionnaire invited open-ended comments about block scheduling from music teachers in each state. Representative responses by state follow.

Kentucky

• We are a small school. It hasn't hurt our enrollment yet, but the jury is still out. . . Our administration has worked hard to schedule the band students.

• I am the only music teacher for the district - teaching band/general music 5-12 - no plans for additional help. I am leaving partly due to block scheduling and lack of high school administrative support for the program.

• So far block scheduling has not affected my program. My program is getting bigger, but it has nothing to do with block scheduling. It may become a problem as I will have more upper classman in 1996-97 . . . The administration has done a good job is scheduling.

• I've been blessed, up to this point, with administrators and counselors who "look out" for the band program. The extra rehearsal time has been beneficial to my program in the short term.

• I'm sure more time is needed to understand the total implications of block scheduling and the effects of "block" on education . . . We will benefit as long as we have administrators who support the music program.

Indiana

• Our administration and school board have tried to accommodate our program with the master schedule to assure our success.

• Students who don't practice at home are suffering due to lack of repetition.

• This schedule creates many problems and conflicts for traveling music teachers especially if they do high school block and elementary traditional.

• Music is only one facet of a total, comprehensive school. Often I hear complaints and criticisms about issues that may negatively affect one discipline while completely revitalizing a dozen others. . . . I have experienced mood/impression swings in a 48-hour period from "I love it - to I hate it - to I don't know."

• Our schedule and I believe block scheduling in general could hurt programs if the administration is not on the lookout for conflicts, especially in smaller schools.

• Many questions are still unanswered.

Michigan

• Since implementation, our achievement level has reached a whole new level. There is now time for theory, music appreciation, and performance as a part of the class structure (small school on a full block).

• This is year five of our block schedule. During this time, I have had only two complete, uninterrupted rehearsals. Our schedule does not work for us (medium school on a modified block).

• Students do come to class more focused. Less class time, yes, but better concentration! We're making it work (large school on a modified block).

• Because we use a modified block where we meet on an alternating day basis, we feel the largest problem is a lack of continuity. Our students are experiencing less literature (large school on a modified block).

• A big problem is losing students to academic classes scheduled against music classes (medium school on a modified block).

• I have enjoyed the creativity that can be developed in a 90 minute period (medium school on a modified block).

• Longer class periods are not as effective as shorter times. It is difficult to stay on task for over an hour with a large group (small school on a modified block).

• Lack of consistency without day to day rehearsals is a problem, especially with underclassmen. Scheduling of multiple music classes is a big problem (large school on a modified block).

Wisconsin

• It seems that at this point our version of modified block is working (large, modified block).

• The choral program has stayed intact because choirs are grade-level choirs. Twenty-six kids signed up for band and didn't get it because of schedule conflicts with other 'singletons' (medium, modified).

• I believe that block scheduling stunts the growth of the music program. What happens if a small school grows to the point where it wants to split an ensemble into two groups. It's not possible with a block schedule (medium, modified block).

• It is very difficult to get kids out of class for lessons (medium, modified block).

• Problems arise with music scheduling when three

performing groups exist. Band & choir share a block -
orchestra is in a 40 minute resource period. The
administration must support a 'no interference' policy
w/orchestra rehearsals to make the music schedule
work (medium, full block).

• We have a modified block schedule with 4 periods for
academics and a shorter 40 minute period for music.
Conflicts are only for those wanting both band and
choir (small, modified block).

• The impact of block scheduling was not so severe as
in other programs because band used to meet MWF for
46 minutes. Now we meet for 92 minutes every other
day (small, modified block).

• Block scheduling was frustrating for me with
students begging to leave band to finish work in other
classes (small, modified block).

• Time with students as individuals or sections has
been lost - especially for H.S. The students you lose are
mostly upper-classman who need or desired advanced
courses. Many compromises have to be made to keep
kids in the program. This takes a *toll* on the large
groups over a period of time (small, modified block).

• Our administration built the schedule around the
music department. We continue to pull students out of
classes for small group lessons. A study hall is opposite
the band/choir block of 90 minutes so that students can
be in both areas. A study hall supervisor was hired so

that the music teachers could give lessons (small, modified block).

• Block scheduling is working for us because of cooperation with administration and guidance dealing with conflicts of needed classes (small, full block).

• Our music block meets daily for 90 minutes, one credit per semester. Students entering grades 10 & 11 are concerned about not getting courses they need, so they are signing up for only one semester. We are trying to find a solution that is workable in our district, such as independent classes during the 2nd half of the block so students take music for the entire year (small, full block).

• Block scheduling has made it very difficult to get students in for ensemble help etc. Choir is no longer offered because 1) block, and 2) more work with elementary classes - 6th grade (small, full block).

• Our scheduling is difficult because there is only one section of each class offered at one time during the day and so I think this would always hurt band and choir enrollment no matter what the schedule (small, modified block).

• Block 8 has been a real headache for lessons. We have A & B days which confuse students. I do not feel that this schedule is conducive to the arts programs in our school (small, modified block).

• Block scheduling does not lend itself to giving lessons

during the day.   Band and choir meet every other day
which I find difficult in correcting problems in rehearsal
or reinforcing positive rehearsals because of at least a
one day wait (small, modified block).

• Modified block scheduling is a must.   While our total
time allowed for 'traditional' ensembles such as concert
band and choir was diminished, we experienced a gain in
'non-traditional' - such as jazz band (both junior and
senior high) as well as women's chorus (small, modified
block).

• It is *essential* that the band/choral/orchestra
directors are able to work together with the
administrators (small, full block).

• Block scheduling reduces the number of choices that
the music students can have (if they were on an 8
period day). The 'brighter' students are once again hurt!
(small, modified block)

CHAPTER 3

Making Block Scheduling Work
Sample Schedules

This chapter presents schedules and descriptions of secondary school music programs in which administrators and music educators have worked together to find solutions for scheduling music performance arts classes. The selected scheduling examples represent several varying types of block scheduling alternatives. No attempt is made to endorse any type or form of scheduling or to suggest that the featured music programs are the best examples of scheduling or that the programs have been able to eliminate all scheduling conflicts. However, the music programs included here do represent outstanding schools which report very successful scheduling cooperation and excelled participation in performing arts classes.

ALTERNATING FOUR-PERIOD DAY -
EIGHT CLASSES

The following is an example of a successful music program on a unique Alternate Day Schedule where band meets every day for a full block period. The scheduling type description, daily schedule, and rationale for offering performance arts classes everyday follows. This description has been submitted by Tanya M. Bromley, Fine Arts Department Chair, Pendleton High School, in Falmouth, Kentucky.

Making Block Scheduling Work
Pendleton High School

In the spring of 1993, the faculty and staff of Pendleton High School, in Falmouth, Kentucky voted to go to an A-B form of block scheduling for the 1994-95 school year. This type of schedule offered students eight year-long classes meeting on alternating days. Students went to classes 1-4 on A days and 5-8 on B days. Each class was 80 minutes long, and there was a lunch block period in the middle of the day for one and a half hours. During this time, students attended enrichment activities which changed every six weeks. Students were required to sign up for an enrichment activity of their choice. A committee of teachers administered the scheduling of these activities.

Naturally this form of schedule threatened the meeting of band class on a daily basis. Fortunately, the school administrators, who were committed to seeing that no subject was adversely affected by the change in scheduling, gave teachers the opportunity to voice their concerns and present them before the school site-based decision making council. We music teachers were careful to put our concerns in writing and have it ready to present to the council. This helped us organize our thoughts and argument for meeting everyday. Our basic premise was that group performance skills took considerably more group time to teach, and current research indicated that skills development was enhanced more by repeated practice than lengthier, less frequent sessions. We calculated the number of minutes currently spent in instruction under the 7-period day and one after-school rehearsal per week and compared that to the number of minutes in instruction under the new schedule. The figures showed that if band met every-other day under block scheduling, we would lose considerable instructional time. Meeting everyday would allow us to maintain the current instructional time and do away with the one after-school rehearsal (with the exception of a few rehearsals prior to a concert or festival performance). This was particularly enticing when it was pointed out that doing away with the weekly after-school rehearsal would reduce conflicts with students participating in sports, academic teams, and after-school jobs. Since there was a possibility of eight periods in the term, two blocks for music performance classes would not adversely affect the music students' scheduling flexibility. The site based council approved the two block allotment for the music performance classes.

A second hurdle appeared when it became evident that the council was not thinking in terms of two credits for the two blocks of time. Again, we went to work preparing our case for two credits for the students. In addition, our booster organization presented their opposition to band students being penalized for credit simply because the class needed to meet everyday. Our premise was based on the fact that our school awarded credit based on *time* and not on the title of a course. For example, students who were interested in business courses could earn many elective course credits in business. Therefore, students interested in music should be allowed to do the same-- even though the course title might not change. Time was time. A key concern of the council was that state regulations might not allow for eight credits in band over a four-year period. After reviewing the state regulations we could see that the state description of studies allowed for four credits in band and four credits in ensemble. Therefore, we simply titled these courses exactly as we delivered them. On A Days, the full band met. Period 4 was titled *Band*. On B Days, the percussion met on Period 7 and the winds meet on Period 8. The course title for these periods was *Instrumental Ensemble*.

We are now into our third year of block scheduling and it has worked very well for our program. The instrumental ensemble days have been a great help in getting more musical instruction and playing opportunity for our percussion students as well as providing for breaking the winds in to sections for their rehearsal. We generally are able to avoid an undue amount of days where percussionist just *sit* because we can work on our wind parts on days when the percussion section is not with us. We have been able to accomplish more, even though we do not have the afternoon rehearsal each week. Freeing up the afternoon has also allowed us to better schedule private lessons for our students.

So far, we have experienced growth in numbers. Since we have only one band (grades 9-12), we do not experience the problem of facility scheduling that occurs in larger schools with multiple ensembles. Our counselors have worked with us in scheduling college prep courses in the morning, and the eight periods have given students more flexibility to take advanced courses and still be able to participate in performing arts classes. Beginning with the 1996-97 school year, Jazz Band has been offered during the activity block. This has allowed us to offer this experience to the students without taking up after-school time or taking up an elective space on their schedule. Future concerns lie in recognizing that other disciplines like math, social studies, and sciences tend to want to add more requirements--especially as they see most students in the school having a lot of extra space for electives. If students are not encumbered with extra requirements, block scheduling can be a real opportunity for students to participate in an array of elective experiences. Teachers of electives need to be vigilant in protecting elective offerings which give students a broader perspective for choosing career paths. These electives enrich their lives for the present and the future.

We believe that our success with block scheduling has hinged upon several factors:

1. The fact that flexibility was increased by using the alternating A/B type of block scheduling. We did not experience the conflict with other courses which might be offered only one semester, etc.
2. The administration was truly concerned with the well-being of all programs and was willing to listen to concerns and explore all possible solutions.
3. There were not multiple ensembles to schedule for the same facility.
4. We presented a logical argument in a "win-win" approach for the students and

we documented the argument so that site
based members could more fully ingest
the ideas presented.

5.   We had the support of parents.

In the spring of 1996, the teachers were asked to
voice their opinion on investigating the standard 4x4
type of block scheduling. After two years of the A/B
alternating day, the teachers affirmed their
satisfaction with the current type of block scheduling.
Many would rather see us return to a seven period day
before going to a strict 4x4.

The following schedule outlines the time line for
the alternating daily schedule.

Pendleton High School
Daily Schedule

8:15 - 9:35	First Block
9:40 - 11:00	Second Block
11:05 - 12:25	Activity/Lunch Interest Block
12:30 - 1:50	Third Block
1:55 - 3:15	Fourth Block

**Report to the Pendleton High School
Site Based Council
Rationale for Offering Band Class
Everyday in Block Scheduling**

submitted by
Tanya M. Bromley

Difference Between Performing Arts Class and Other Skills-Development Classes

Skills-development classes focus on the development of individual skills: i.e.: typing, computer-techniques, cooking, sewing, playing an instrument.

Performing groups take individual skills (playing an instrument) and coordinate those individual skills to create a new entity--band, chorus, theatre, etc. A clarinet player might perform as a soloist, however; a new set of skills are required for performing in a small ensemble, a band, an orchestra, etc.

Although individual skills can be practiced independently, group skills must be developed through group interaction. This is why band or chorus is more than collaborative learning. The collaboration is not a method to achieve an end--

it is the end itself. The quality of the product, then, is not only determined by the quality of the performers--it is determined by the effectiveness of their interaction and response to each other. Musical group skills include: balancing, blending, tuning, precision, and group stylistic interpretation. These skills cannot be simulated at an independent level. This is why effective teaching of group techniques simply demands more group time together.

Why School Bands Take More Preparation Than Other Performing Group Classes

Most other performing groups (theatre, chorus) utilize the coordination of techniques which people use everyday--body movement, speaking, vocalizing. Bands--particularly at the middle and secondary school level are made up of students who play an instrument which is *outside* of the body. Therefore, an additional element is added to the challenge of performing. The student must learn to utilize facial and other muscles which are often-times not highly developed. In addition, the student must develop a breathing technique which is not the same as the normal breathing process. Each student must also learn a fingering system which requires a different fingering or muscular position for as many as forty different notes! In an average band, there are 12 different fingering systems and as many as 18 different instruments. Added to this is the fact that the student must learn to read and interpret a system of pitch and rhythmic symbols. The band students must learn to develop these independent skills as well as the group skills mentioned above. Often times there are as many as 25 different parts being played at one time in order to perform a single piece of music.

The bottom line is that instrumental development simply takes a lot of time. The evaluation of the same must be of an interactive nature--the teacher must actually see and hear what the student is doing, Again, time.

Review of the Present Time Allotted to Band

At present, the band practices everyday during school and one afternoon per week after school. This is already cut to minimum so that our students can participate as much as possible in other activities.

5 Fifty-four minute periods = 270 minutes class time
1 Ninety minute after school = 90 minutes after school
          Total per wk = 300 x 2 (weeks) = 720

With the proposed new schedule, a two-week period would yield:

5 Eighty minute periods = 400 minutes
1 Ninety minute per 2 wk = 180 minutes
          Total two week time = 580
          Total loss = 140 minutes

To regain this loss, we would have to have an extra hour rehearsal after school **each** week. *(Keep in mind, we are already working at minimum capacity to produce a group that students can take pride in and feel a sense of accomplishment and self-worth).*

> Band meeting everyday on the new block schedule would yield 800 minutes per every two weeks.

By meeting everyday we would not need afternoon rehearsals. We can continue to maintain the quality in our instruction *and* free up afternoon time for our students to participate in other activities and prepare their studies. This is even more in the interest of our band students when one considers that in addition to the time our students spend developing their own talent and musical interests, they spend between 60-75 hours per year providing entertainment for ball games, parades, civic and school ceremonies.

How Will This Affect Students Scheduling Options?

Basically, band students will have as many options as they have now. There would be the possibility to take as many as six subjects and band (a total of seven). A student who does not take band, would have the option of eight subjects, however; time to prepare for eight different subjects might cause one to frown on this and encourage a study hall. Even though the band student's schedule would be full, there would be one less preparation. This may turn out to be an advantage for the band students--particularly those brighter students who do not want a study hall and might tend to *overload their plate.*

Rationale for Awarding Two Credits for the Two-Block Instrumental Class

Recently, the PHS Site-Based council approved the meeting of instrumental music (band) for two blocks in the new block schedule. The decision was truly in the spirit of the Kentucky Education Reform Act (KERA) and site-based management, because it gave those most directly involved in the instruction an opportunity to make recommendations, it recognized the uniqueness of the collaborative learning process and the time needed for student interaction in the class, and it did not let schedule dictate or hamper the best form of delivery. Most of all, the decision was made in light of what would help students maintain a rewarding and successful experience.

An area of concern developed when the council allowed only one block of credit for a two-block instructional period. Under the current accrediting policy of PHS, credits are awarded based on the number of blocks a student spends in a course. Courses which meet for one block for one semester receive 1/2 credit. Those courses meeting a block for a full year receive one credit. Credits are not weighted, but are based on class time needed for delivery. In order to be consistent with this policy, a class that meets for two blocks during the year should receive two credits. This does not imply that the class is more important or takes more preparation outside of school than another class, it simply recognizes that the student has invested two blocks, or credits, of instructional time in the course. To award less, would be in effect to weight the course adversely.

Another area of concern was that the awarding of two credits for the two blocks would seem to have been disproportionate allocation of elective credits to any one class. Although the band course generically goes under the title "band," one must keep in mind that it is a multi-grade course in which the curriculum is graduated for freshmen through seniors (accomplished through multi-level theory and history workbooks, solo and ensemble literature, and level-specific playing examinations). The music literature is presented in a four-year cycle. Therefore, if a student is interested in instrumental music, it is not any more disproportionate to put 8 credits in band than it is to elect 8 credits of various business and marketing courses.

Under the PHS Comprehensive Diploma, 8 electives are required for graduation (one of which must be a fine arts credit). However, with block scheduling, 16 total elective blocks are available. The enrichment diploma allows for 18 blocks of electives, and the standard diploma allows for 20. As one can see, there is lots of elective credit flexibility in all three diplomas. To put a limit on how many electives in any one area of interest a student might have would seem to negate the meaning of the word *elective.*

A primary concern is whether 8 credits in band is allowable under the present state Program of Studies. Fortunately, the instructional delivery for band at PHS is set up in such a manner that it is not only allowable, but 2 credits, for the two-block schedule proposed, would be, by state standards, *technically correct.* Currently, our band members meet separately as two ensembles: percussion class and wind class. Under our course catalog, the percussion students receive instrumental ensemble credit--not band credit. Under the proposed two-block schedule, percussion and wind classes would continue to meet separately on an A day and jointly, as a band, on a B day. The Program of Studies allows 4 credits in band and 4 credits in instrumental ensemble. Because our wind class is team-taught, the group regularly breaks into sections, and even smaller ensembles. Under the proposed schedule, this will be extensive. Under our current course catalog, percussion students receive an ensemble credit for the percussion class (course #2837) and can take the band class (course #2834). Under our current course catalog and proposed schedule, awarding a percussionist two credits for the two blocks *is already perfectly acceptable.* Technically, the only change needed is that the wind class course catalog number needs to be more appropriately changed to the ensemble number 2837 and the catalogs need to read:

Band #2834
Instrumental Ensemble #2837

In conclusion, one must keep in mind that informed parents, teachers, and administrators know that the number of credits allotted per blocks of time is not necessarily an indication of value or worth. In the perception of most parents and students, credits are payment for class time spent. One of the selling points of block scheduling was that teachers would have more *compensated* time for planning. Should the students expect less compensation for their time?

I can justify the students giving up an elective choice in order to have less after-school obligations because it frees them to more fully participate in other extra-curricular offerings. I do not feel that I can justify giving up an elective choice and a credit while other students are being fully compensated. There are some extremely dedicated students who would take any favorite course if *no* credit was given. But it takes many students, with varying degrees of commitment and interest, to make any good group or team. In the band program, or any other team program, these children play a valuable part in filling out the team and making it a great experience for everyone. I truly believe that our band will lose students who do not feel equally compensated for their time.

(On a personal note, there is nothing self-serving about this request. It would have been a lot less of a headache to take the two-block time with one credit and run with it. But that is *not* student-centered. Awarding two credits for two blocks of time will not hurt a single child in our school, but I can give you the names of the students who will be directly hurt if they are not compensated equally for their two blocks of time).

Respectfully submitted,
Tanya M. Bromley
May 23, 1994

THE 4X4 BLOCK SCHEDULE

The following is an example of a successful music program on a 4x4 Block Schedule where band and chorus meets every day for a full block period for the entire semester. The scheduling type description and daily schedule follows. This description has been submitted by Jon Milleman, Band Director, Angola High School Band, Angola, Indiana and has appeared in a similar form in the May/June 1996 issue of the *BD Guide* of Tempe, Arizona, Volume 10 #5 (pp. 28-31).

Background

Angola High School in Angola, Indiana is located in Steuben County. It is the farthest northeast county in Indiana. Our city is the county seat of Steuben County and the largest community in the county. Our high school has approximately 850 students. Students' backgrounds range from low income families to high income families and we reflect this diversity in the performing arts program. Parents and community view the school as responsible and the level of trust between the school and the community is high. Our band booster organization is strong and growing (at this time we have no external choir booster organization).

The band program at Angola offers concert band, jazz band, marching band, pep band, winter color guard, solo and ensemble participation, and a small number of private lessons.   Enrollment in band requires participation in marching band, concert band and pep band.   Lessons, solo and ensemble, jazz band, and winter guard are optional. The choir program offers two ensembles divided by ability level.   There is no orchestra program at Angola High School.

Planning the 4x4 Schedule

Our principal, Dr. Rex Bolinger began the process of examining alternate schedules in 1992.   Since then our staff and students have gone through an extensive examination of possible alternate schedules that would help lower the daily number of students per teacher, lessen the stress on the teacher and the student, and enhance student learning. This task would have been enough.   However, I wanted to stand firm in our program to preserve our strength as a band program, as well as maintain our requirements for participation in concert and marching band. One key to our success in implementing our current schedule was the commitment from the administration and the scheduling committee to maintain the current level of success in our strong programs.   I was consulted through every step of the process. The philosophy in dealing with music was "let's not try to fix something that is not broken."

Planning the schedule also included the use of research by Robert Lynn Canady. Dr. Canady visited our school in 1994 and opened the eyes of our staff to the enormous possibilities of alternate schedules. One of the important points of his discussions was the need to *tailor a schedule to the unique characteristics of your school.* Use the research, learn from other schools, but ultimately do what is right for *your* situation. If that means you do nothing, you at least are stronger from a careful examination of your current schedule.

Old Schedule

Until this school year, we were on a seven period day. Students in performance classes took band/choir plus six other classes or band/choir plus five classes and a study period. Jazz Band met in the morning outside of the school day for no credit. We do not offer a jazz or show choir. (Figure 1)

OLD ANGOLA SCHEDULE (Figure 1)

Band	Class	Class	Class	Class	Class	Class

Our New Schedule

Our new band schedule utilizes the full 90 minute block of time for the first nine weeks as full band rehearsal. (Figure 2) This is during the marching band season when there is typically a great deal more rehearsal time required of the students outside of the school day.

During marching band, we rehearse before school on Monday and Wednesday mornings beginning at 7:00 AM. On the weeks of ISSMA Regional and State Finals we rehearse on Monday, Tuesday and Wednesday mornings at 7:00 AM. We dismiss the students from the morning rehearsal at 9:30 AM. This gives us a 2 1/2 hour rehearsal on these mornings. Of course we still see the students for 90 minutes on Tuesday, Thursday and Friday (we net about 80 minutes on these days factoring transit time and equipment concerns). We also rehearse on Thursday evening (one night per week) to allow our staff to rehearse with the entire band.

First Nine Weeks (Figure 2)

Band	Class	Class	Class
90 minutes	90 minutes	90 minutes	90 minutes

Band students receive 1 full credit for the first nine weeks. This is because in the 4x4 schedule a nine week grading period is the same as a semester in the old schedule.

During the second, third and fourth nine weeks, the band splits the first 90 minute block between concert band and jazz band. For the first 45 minutes of the block, the band meets in concert band. At the end of the 45 minutes the students in jazz band move to another rehearsal space (the stage in our case) and rehearse for the second 45 minutes. Those students who are not in jazz band go to seminar. (Figure 3)

Second, Third and Fourth Nine Weeks (Figure 3)

Band-45 min Seminar or Jazz -45 min	Class	Class	Class

Seminar is much like a traditional study hall only it has the feature of being supervised by a classroom teacher. There are classroom teachers supervising seminars during each block. For the student, this means that there is tutoring available in each subject from a classroom teacher. It may not be the teacher they have in a given subject but a teacher in each subject is available.

The feature of the seminar is what allowed us to utilize 45 minutes for jazz band. Also, the seminars give Dr. Bolinger a place to locate students that need removed from a class for any reason. Students can be moved to seminar rooms for make-up examinations or other independent work. The seminar also was important to the administration because moving to the 4x4 schedule did not require additional staff.

We also allow the winter color guard members to stay during the second 45 minutes. They work on cleaning their equipment work and go over parts of their show. These students are required to log their practice time and the captains must sign the practice log to verify the fact that the work was completed.

Also, because we are in a team teaching situation in all bands, my assistant director uses the second 45 minutes to coach solo and ensemble students and work with various sections of the concert band on upcoming concert or contest music. We accomplish this by publishing a seminar schedule at least a week in advance. This gives the students the opportunity to plan ahead. They will know in advance the days that they are expected to stay for the full 90 minutes. During the week of concerts we typically have the full band stay for the entire 90 minutes. Students must come to my office before band starts to sign out of seminar. We then take the list of students to the seminar supervisor so she will know who to expect during seminar. The choir director publishes a list of choir members so the office can divide the seminar classes.

Typical Weekly Rehearsal Schedule

Time	Mon	Tues	Wed	Thurs	Fri
1st 45 min	Full Concert Band	Full Concert Band	Full Concert Band	Full Concert Band	Full Concert Band
2nd 45 min	Full Jazz Band Rehearsal	Jazz Band Saxes & Rhythm	Full Jazz Band Rehearsal	Jazz Band Brass & Rhythm	Full Jazz Band Rehearsal
	Solo & Ensemble Students with Asst. Director	Concert Band Brass with Asst. Director	Solo & Ensemble Students with Asst. Director	Concert Band Brass with Asst. Director	Solo & Ensemble Students with Asst. Director

One reason that this is attractive to band students is they are able to have 45 minutes of study time daily (something that my students say is better than the long 90 minute study period). Then the student is able to fill up the remaining three blocks with classes allowing them to take their requirements as well as electives.

I counsel my freshmen to take Physical Education during the first nine weeks along with another low homework class. This greatly reduces the stress of dealing with the transition into high school along with the busy marching band schedule. Our guidance department counsels all students to balance the low homework classes with the high homework classes.

Remember since nine weeks is the same as a semester, the old traditional semester classes only meet for nine weeks. Therefore students are able to take two classes during the same block of time within the same semester. I have freshmen in band that are enrolled in 7 other classes. (Figure 4)

Sample Band Student Schedule (Figure 4)

First Semester		Second Semester
First 9 Weeks	**Second 9 Weeks**	
Band 90 minutes	Band 45 minutes Seminar or Jazz 45 minutes	Band 45 minutes Seminar or Jazz Band 45 minutes
P.E.	P.E.	Science
English	English	Math
Computer App.	Basic Art	Foreign Language

Students are given credit and a grade for band.

They receive 1/2 credit each for the second, third and fourth nine weeks unless they are in jazz band in which case they receive 1 credit for each nine weeks. Students in jazz band will receive 4 credits and non-jazz band students receive 2 1/2 credits.

The choir schedule is essentially the same. However, the choir meets in a different block of time. There are other alternatives available within the 4x4 schedule for the performing arts. Choir could be scheduled during the same block as bands for some schools to assist students that wish to do both. Because we share teachers with the middle school, this is very difficult. Also, the choir or orchestra schedule could utilize an A day B day alternating schedule. Choirs could then meet on opposite days for 90 minutes each. The block could be split 30/60 or 45/45. Some students from the upper level choir could stay and work with the second choir students if they had all homework completed and did not need to attend seminar.

In programs that do not share teachers with the middle school, the possibility of backing various ensembles against each other on the schedule exists. Jazz band could be scheduled with orchestra and the orchestra could share the students to fill in the wind section of full orchestra.

Why Block Scheduling is Working

There are several reasons why I believe that this schedule is not harmful to the music program. Even more important, there are reasons why I believe that this schedule is helpful to our program.

- *The Administration was aware of our success as a program and made a conscious effort to protect that success*
- *The scheduling committee of teachers communicated with the band director throughout the entire process*
- *Angola H.S. researched and studied schedules for three years before implementing. Many of our questions and concerns were addressed* **before** *implementation*
- *The administration agreed to preserve the current policy requiring a full year of participation in band*
- *We informed band parents about the new schedule in advance. We sent pamphlets to the home and we held special band parent meetings on the subject of scheduling*
- *We have an eighth grade information night each year before scheduling to inform*
  Our parent organization is strong and they asked questions throughout the entire process
- *We are able to offer jazz band for credit and meet every day*

- *The use of the second 45 minutes during concert band makes solo & ensemble coaching available during the school day eliminating some of the after school scheduling conflicts*
- *Private lessons can be taught during the second 45 minutes*
- *Instructional videos and special guests can be brought in for the entire 90 minute block*

DO'S
- *Be involved in the change from the beginning*
- *Ask many questions about the schedule. A schedule that works at one school, may not be the best for you. Identify the areas of strength and tailor the schedule to your unique characteristics.*
- *Ask questions about the reasoning in each scheduling decision*
- *Keep your parents informed about the process*
- *Keep your students informed about the process, being honest will give you more credibility*
- *Make sure that you can live with the amount of rehearsal time that you will have in the new schedule*

DON'TS
- *Assume anything that you want is understood*
- *Appear inflexible*
- *Let the situation happen to you*

- *Trust someone to convey your message or concerns -
  Do it yourself*
- *Misinform your students throughout the process. If
  you don't know all of the facts, don't discuss the
  schedule in class.*
- *Make enemies*
- *Take sides in the discussions; Take the side of the
  band*

At this point, we are very pleased with the flexibility of the schedule. We are able to require a full year of participation without disrupting the students' diploma track or AP track schedule. Students have morning rehearsals which requires less outside rehearsal time (we actually gained about 1 1/2 hours more rehearsal time in marching band).

We have had very little problems with students' schedules. There is only one "singleton" course scheduled at the same time as band. It is not a prerequisite course and Dr. Bolinger advised us that he would have moved the course if he was aware of it. Our numbers have stayed essentially the same since last year. In fact we grew by approximately 6 students (in coming freshmen). I am confident that the lines of communication are open between the band, the committee, and the administration.

We are happy to meet with other directors or fax

information to schools regarding our 4x4 schedule. Remember: be involved from the beginning. Schedules like the 4x4 are *going* to happen most places. Help make the change happen *with* you, not *to* you.

From the Principal
Dr. Rex W. Bolinger
Angola High School

Jon Milleman has developed a model for successful connections with instrumental music programs and the 4-Block schedule. It has worked extremely well at Angola High School. Other fine arts programs, such as vocal music, have chosen to follow an A-day or B-day schedule within the 4-Block, which also works well. Both depend upon the seminar/tutoring periods developed with Angola's schedule.

Superintendent of Schools
The Metropolitan School District of Steuben County
Dr. Oren Skinner
400 S. Martha Street
Angola, Indiana 46703
(219) 665-2854

HYBRID SCHEDULE -
LONG AND SHORT CLASSES

The following is an example of a successful music program on a unique Hybrid Schedule. Descriptions of this form of scheduling, the school music program, the planning process, why block scheduling is working, advantages and disadvantages of the scheduling with performance arts classes, and suggestions for other music educators follows. This description has been submitted by:

Judy Moore, Chair
Music Department,
Eleanor Roosevelt High School
7601 Hanover Parkway
Greenbelt, Maryland 20770.

Eleanor Roosevelt High School and
Block Scheduling

Eleanor Roosevelt has over 3060 students and is one of the largest schools in the state. The school contains a magnet program and a comprehensive program. The magnet program is geared for science and technology. Eight-hundred of these students are in the science and technology program, referred to as "tech students." The others are in the comprehensive program, "comp students."

Eleanor Roosevelt has developed a modified

scheduling plan named the "Hybrid Schedule" as it is made up of double and single mod classes. The singled mod classes are 45 minutes every day for a full year. The double mod classes are 90 minutes everyday for one semester, half the year. Music classes, along with other production classes meet for the full year as single mod classes. A sample schedule is shown below of a senior science and technology student. The student takes one class before the actual school day begins, called zero period. The student has two double mod classes and is enrolled in two upper level music classes, band and choir.

Sample Daily Student Schedule

0	1	2	3	4	5	6	7	8
8:15-9:00	9:30 11:05		11:10-11:55	12:00-12:45	12:50-1:35	1:40-2:25	2:30-4:05	
Spanish 2	Physics AP Gov.	1st Sem. 2nd Sem.	Lunch	Wind Ensemb.	Pre Calculus	Chamber Choir	English Ger 3	1st Sem. 2nd Sem.

Description of School Music Program

The Eleanor Roosevelt Music Department has a core program of band, choir, guitar/piano, marching band, music survey, and orchestra (this year we have added marching band). Five full time music teachers teach over 700 students in the music program. There are five levels of band, four choirs, three levels of guitar/piano, marching band, music survey, and three levels of orchestra. Extra-curricular music activities are many. Students in band, choir, and orchestra are eligible to perform in solo and ensemble festival and audition for county and state performing groups. The after-school performing groups include Jazz Band, Dixieland Band, Flute Choir, String Quartet, and Music Theater.

Each of the band, choir, and orchestra groups perform for the public three times per year. County music festivals are traditionally attended by all the performing groups. One or two groups are selected each year to compete in a nationally or internationally-recognized music festival. Many students in the core groups perform with outside music groups as well. The Music Department receives frequent requests for student groups to perform at county functions.

Since the school moved from a traditional eight period day to the Hybrid Schedule, the music program has experienced no more conflicts than usual. Students in some cases must make a choice between music or an upper level class. This was also the case before the Hybrid Schedule was adopted. The curriculum coordinator, scheduling coordinator, and science and technology coordinator work to eliminate conflicts. The computer driven schedule is given a preliminary run in July. Conflicts are noted. Then the hand scheduling begins. In some cases irresolvable conflicts arise. The student and parent are notified and asked to make a choice.

Block Scheduling and the Music Program

The music schedule is carefully planned to allow students to take more than one upper level music class. Both Symphony and Chamber Orchestras draw back from the band for wind and percussion. Thus the classes are scheduled back to back. However, Chamber Choir meets a different period allowing some of the very talented students to participate in all three upper level music ensembles. The schedule for the music offerings and teacher assignments follows on the next page.

The Music Schedule

0	1	2	3	4	5	6	7	8
8:15-9:00	9:30-10:15	10:20-11:05	11:10-11:55	12:00-12:45	12:50-1:35	1:40-2:25	2:30-3:15	3:20-4:05
Teacher A	Sectional	Planning	Women's Choir	Lunch	Sectional	Chamber Choir	Gospel Choir	Section.
Teacher B	Sectional	Planning	Symphony Orch.	Chamber Orch.	Lunch	Sectional	Concert Orch.	Beginning Guitar/Piano
Teacher C	Concert Choir	Planning	Intermediate Guitar/Piano	Lunch	Advan. Guitar/Piano	Beginning Guitar/Piano	Sectional	Section.
Teacher D *also teaches March. Band	Not in Building	Beginning Guitar/Piano	Sectional	Lunch	Concert Band 3	Concert Band 2	Planning	Section.
Teacher E	Sectional	Planning	Symphonic Band	Wind Ensem.	Lunch	Concert Band 1	Sectional	Music Survey (first sem.)

Please note that Marching Band meets Tuesday, Thursday, and Friday from 4:15-6:00. Students in this class receive one fine arts credit.

Orchestra class has no winds enrolled. The winds who audition into orchestra are permitted by the band teacher to leave band and go to orchestra class on prearranged days. The full orchestra frequently rehearses after school on some days.

The Planning Process

A thorough description of the planning process involved in creating the Hybrid Schedule is presented in the article "The Hybrid Schedule: Scheduling to the Curriculum." The article by Gerald L. Boarman, principal, and Barbara S. Kirkpatrick, curriculum coordinator, appears in the May 1995 issue of the NASSP Bulletin (pp. 42-52). Highlights follow.

1991-1992

Year	Happening	Result
1991-1992	Zero Period first offered Zero Period begins at 8:15 and ends at 9:00. The regular school day begins at 9:25 with announcements.	Some teachers could begin the work day earlier and leave earlier. Students could elect more courses giving more schedule space for electives.

1992-1993 (Spring Semester)

Year	Happening	Result
1992-1993 (Spring Semester)	PART I: Project 120 120 academically talented students were Placed in double mod periods in selected subjects. PART II: A Day B Day 60 students were placed in an A Day B Day format for selected, paired classes. For instance, engineering and chemistry were paired for these students. On A Day the students had 90 minutes of engineering. On B Day the same went to chemistry for the same period.	Project 120: teachers had less students in a day. Students had fewer subjects in a day. Some teaching time was saved by avoiding the passing from class to class and setting down a new class every period. PART II: A Day B Day Both chemistry and engineering now had more time for labs. However, these teachers still had the same work load. A group of teachers from each department in the school visited other schools who use the "4 period Block day."

1993-1994

Year	Happening	Result
1993-1994	Double mod classes offered to 250 students in matched pairs: English/social studies and science/math. Faculty vote on moving to double mod format (Block Scheduling)	Teachers of these double mods seemed to feel a reduced work load with seeing fewer students each quarter. The faculty voted against going to a double mod format at this time. Production/ performance class teachers explained that meeting their classes for only half the year would destroy the building process of the current program.

January 1994

Year	Happening	Result
January 1994	The Hybrid Schedule developed.	The faculty advisory committee met. The group solicited opinions from all the departments in the school. The Hybrid Schedule became a reality. Double mod classes were offered in the major subjects excluding AP courses. However, it was not possible for all major subject classes to be selected in the double mod format.

1995-1996

Year	Happening	Result
1995-1996	More classes are added to the double mod offerings.	Music, Drama, Art, and Yearbook are among the subjects still in the single mod format. Although some scheduling problems arise; they do not seem to be over-whelming.

Why Block Scheduling is Working

The school is quite large. Almost 3,100 students attend daily classes. Because of the size of the student population, different offerings can be accommodated. As stated above, the administrative staff understands the importance of the arts and the elective program to the health of a school. Because of this, the master schedule is designed to reduce conflicts. Many students are given individual attention to resolve scheduling dilemmas. In a few cases teachers themselves agree on how it is possible to share a student between two classes. It must be emphasized that the sharing of students is rare.

Roosevelt music teachers work hand in hand with the guidance and scheduling departments to place each music student appropriately. At the end of the school year band, choir, and orchestra students are auditioned and placed in groups for the coming year. Before the school year is finished the guidance department knows where each music student should be placed. The music teachers do come to school at various times in the summer to check on the scheduling progress.

Occasionally a student will elect not to continue in music due to conflicts such as graduation requirements not met, science and tech-internship, or upper-level language conflict.

The Advantages and Disadvantages of the Hybrid Schedule

ADVANTAGES
1. Students have a broad array of choices.
2. Teachers of double mods perceive a smaller class size.
3. Scheduling conflicts seem to be about the same as

before the Hybrid Schedule was adopted.

4. Production classes see students all year. Teachers can plan sequential skill development activities such as festivals and concerts at the end of the year.

5. There is less hall traffic.

6. Lab classes have time to complete activities.

DISADVANTAGES

1. Teachers of double mods are forced to plan each lesson more carefully. Problems occur when double mod teachers must be out of the building because of illness or meetings.

THE EMBEDDED BLOCK SCHEDULE

The following is an example of creative scheduling using both a full and modified semester schedule. Included is the rationale for change, planning, implementation, and improvement with the high school restructuring plan. A description of the "embedded" program as it relates to music is presented. This description has been submitted by Mr. Luther W. Fennell, Principal, Thomas A. Edison High School, 5801 Franconia Road, Alexandria, Virginia 22310.

The following document serves as an exemplary outline of the procedures in implementing and planning change with high school scheduling. This document is presented with permission and gratitude is expressed to Mr. Fennell, the faculty and staff of Thomas A Edison High School, and the administration of the Fairfax County Public Schools.

THOMAS A EDISON HIGH SCHOOL
Restructured School Day
Rationale for Change, Planning, Implementation, and Improvement

Thomas A. Edison implemented a restructured school schedule beginning in the 1994-1995 school year. This document is an overview of the rationale for change, planning, implementation, and improvement of the restructured model selected by Edison High School. Data collected during Phase I (1994-95) and Phase II (1995-96) of the implementation is included. In addition, improvements for Phase III (1996-97) are discussed.

Rationale for Change

There are several factors that have motivated hundreds of schools across the United States to restructure school time. The reasons Edison High School decided to restructure included concerns about:

- student clients per teacher (up to 150 students per day more)

- teacher contacts per student (seven per day)

- learner transitions per day (seven per day)

- inadequate daily planning time for teachers

- student attendance rates

- student achievement rates

- instructional time lost due to class changes and transitions

- too little time for individualized instruction

- many daily preparations for teachers and students each day

- lack of time for teachers to maintain close parental

contact

- inadequate class time for implementing critical-thinking and problem-solving strategies

- inadequate time to learn new technologies for improved instruction and achievement

- too little time for implementing varied teaching strategies for varied learners

- too little opportunity for students to pursue in-depth study in a field due to limited opportunities for selecting electives

An Overview of the Edison Plan

In addition to addressing these reasons for change, the Edison Semester Plan accomplishes the following:

- Most students prepare for only four classes during a grading period as compared to seven.

- Teachers have a maximum of three preparations for any grading period (down from five).

- Most teacher student loads are reduced from up to 150 students per grading period to an average of 70-75.

- The number of resources needed, such as textbooks, microscopes, and graphing calculators, are reduced resulting in financial savings.

- Computer labs and facility resources are more effectively used by more students over the course of a year.

- With classes meeting every day, forward momentum is more easily maintained allowing students to progress more rapidly in their studies; less time is needed for review from the previous class meeting.

- Classes meet for one hour each during weather-related delayed openings.

The main components of the Edison Restructured School Day are:

- The school year is divided into two, 90-day sessions called Fall and Spring Terms.

- Most one credit classes meet for 90 minutes each day for one term.

- Some classes meet every other day all year and are called **embedded** classes.

- **Embedded** classes include production classes such as Band and Yearbook, AP classes, and courses such as Physical Education that are used for balancing options.

- Students are able to elect an eighth course, allowing them to earn up to 32 credits toward graduation.

- Teachers may teach three classes each semester with a daily 90-minute planning period.

Planning

Edison High School began its study of restructuring at the recommendations of the Area I Superintendent of the Fairfax County Public Schools beginning in 1992, two years before the plan was eventually implemented. This effort included collaboration among the following stake holders:

- Edison faculty and staff
- Students of Edison High School
- Parents from the Edison community including parents of Twain Middle School students

The effort was organized around a central steering committee and seven subcommittees each of which included representatives from the above mentioned groups. The subcommittees were:

- Staff Development
- Achievement Center
- Master Schedule
- Evaluation and Research
- Communications
- Mobility
- Individual Professional Responsibility (IPR)

The steering committee and subcommittees researched school restructuring through the following:

- Consultations with experts in the field of school restructuring including Dr. Lynn Canady and Dr. Michael Rettig

- Consultations with members of the FCPS

leadership team including Janie Smith from the
Department of Instructional Services, and Dr. Don
Sheldon, Area I Superintendent

- School visitations to numerous restructured schools
  in Virginia and Maryland

- Conference calls to various schools and professional
  organizations

- Library research on school restructuring

The Edison Model consists of the best parts of the
multitude of restructured plans studied. It truly came
from within the school and community as a bottom-up
approach to site-based decision making. The final plan
addressed the concerns expressed by members of the
Edison and Twain communities, the Edison Staff, the
student body, and members of the school leadership
team. This information was solicited, synthesized, and
shared through the following:

- Visitations to other schools were followed by
  debriefing sessions open to the faculty and
  community.

- Edison's visitors to other schools submitted written
  responses to questions and observations.

- An overview of the plan was presented at two
  community forums attended by hundreds of Twain
  and Edison parents, representatives from the FCPS
  school board, and the FCPS leadership team. A

free-flowing dialog was established at the meetings between parents and committee members; written feedback was solicited and responses were provided.

- Information was continually shared with the community through newsletters and updates.

- Personal responses by phone were made to community members with questions.

- Faculty meetings included discussions where concerns were shared.

- Over seventy percent of the faculty approved implementation of the final plan through a faculty vote.

- Dr. Sheldon, the Area I Superintendent, approved the final plan.

Specific parts of the final restructured plan that addressed concerns of stake holders:

- Embedded classes

- Scheduling of teacher assignments

- Unencumbered 90 minutes of teacher planning every day

- Assessment and transition of mobile students (which had never been done before)

- New and improved staff-development opportunities

- Program evaluation

Staff Development

Staff development played a critical role in the implementation of Edison's restructured school schedule. During Spring, 1994, key areas of need for teacher-training were identified through a faculty survey. Based on the results of the survey, a comprehensive staff-development plan was developed for Edison (and subsequently adopted by DIS as a model for Block Scheduling Staff Development). The plan provides not only pre-implementation training, but on-going opportunities for training and support. The plan focuses on improving academic achievement, school achievement, school climate, and interpersonal relationships within school and includes a variety of formats:

* Motivational presentations (Spring 1994)

* Formal presentations by national expert

* Full-day faculty training (2 days, August, 1994)

* Half-day departmental retreat

* Day of Reflection

* Curriculum improvement improvement writing projects

Currently, staff-development activities during the 1995-96 school year have focused on teacher projects which rewrite curriculum in demonstrated areas of instructional need. For example, the trigonometry and math analysis course is being analyzed and rewritten due to the significant number of student failures during last school year. Similarly, the Ninth Grade Planning Team has studied the AVID *Study Skills Curriculum* in order to facilitate the adjustment of ninth graders to the academic demands of high schools. Both projects include teacher-training components.

Research and Evaluation

The Research and Evaluation Committee of Edison High School was formed in January 1994 as part of Edison's Restructured School Day Initiative. The committee was charged with two primary goals:

- Plan and conduct a literature review on restructured schools and present the findings to the Edison community.

- Plan and implement program evaluation of Edison's restructured school initiative.

After and extensive study of over 150 articles, books and other references, the committee was able to share a clear picture of "what works and what doesn't work." After a six month research period, and using the *Edison School Plan* as a guide, the following questions focused the development of our research design:

- Has student achievement improved?

- Has student attendance improved?

- Has the number of disciplinary referrals decreased?

- Has the number of student drop-outs declined?

- Has the school climate improved?

- How well has our school met the RSD program outcomes?

Next, the Research and Evaluation Committee determined the best way to answer these questions. Since survey research is used in education for a wide variety of purposes including program evaluation, the committee determined that survey research was the most appropriate type of research for evaluating Edison's program outcomes.   In contrast, the committee decided that **student outcomes** would be measured quantitatively by comparing school data on academic achievement, attendance, and discipline.

Subjects
The committee decided to collect information from three groups: students, faculty and parents. All persons in each group were surveyed (students, N=610; teachers, N=88; and parents, N=300), with the exception of the parent group. In this group, 300 parents were identified by a stratified random sample

(selected from students in 9th, 10th, and 11th grade classes, 93-94 school year).

Instrumentation

Unique surveys were developed for each group (student, teacher, and parent); each survey addressed all twelve program outcomes:

- Increased variety of instructional strategies

- Increased quality of student work

- Increased homework completion

- Increased time-on-task for all students

- Decreased number of discipline referrals

- Increased use of instructional technology

- Decrease in the number of students seen by teachers per day

- Increased parental contact

- Enhanced staff development

- Increased unencumbered planning time

- Less fragmentation in the school day

- Improved school climate

Procedures

After the survey questions were developed, surveys were critically reviewed, edited, and pretested by a wide range of stake holders--RSD committee members, school principal, students, and a parent. Opinions about program outcomes were measured twice--the first set of surveys were conducted during June 1994 prior to the 94-95 implementation school year; a second set of surveys were conducted in May 1995. Responses were tallied from six separate sets of surveys. Percentages were reported for PRE and POST implementation surveys for each question. The Office of Research and Program Evaluation provided technical assistance during the summer of 1995 in order to determine statistical significance.

Results

Using statistical tests significant at the .10 level, there is a 90 percent certainty that the findings are not due to chance. Although many positive changes were noted in the pre-post results, the focus here is only on statistically significant change which was shown in eight of twelve program outcome areas. Furthermore, significant changes were found among all three groups; teachers, students, and parents (*Appendix A in the original document outlines statistically significant findings in more detail*).

Of particular note are the findings that

- teachers feel they now have time to work individually with students (from 6% pre-always to 21% post-always);

- teachers feel they have adequate planning time (from 2% pre-always to 15% post-always; from 15% pre-often to 28% post-often);

- parents feel that they are satisfied with their student's behavior at school (from 29% pre-always to 49% post-always); and

- students feel that they complete homework assignments (from 7% pre-always to 29% post-always).

Although parents reported less contact with their student's teachers (from 18% pre-always to 2% post-always), this is consistent with, according to Virginia State Department of Education personnel, findings from studies at Atlee High School (VA). We hypothesize that since parents have greater satisfaction with their student's behavior, there is less perception of need for contact with school personnel.

In summary, this qualitative study along with comparative quantitative data suggest that the Edison community has developed a unique model which should provide steady, measurable improvement in all program outcomes when studied from a longitudinal perspective.

Phase I And II Implementation Data

Some important facts about Edison High School:

- Accredited by the Commission on Secondary Schools Southern Association of Colleges and Schools.

- The highest average daily attendance rate among FCPS Area I High Schools.

- Edison has over 40 clubs and organizations and participates in all Virginia High School League Athletics.

- Students are consistently among the top two in the number of awards at the Fairfax County Regional Science Fair and in 1996 was a Westinghouse Semi-Finalist.

- The home of the Virginia State Debate Champions.

- A strong performing arts program which is recognized as one of Northern Virginia's finest.

- The school newspaper "Edison Current," and annual yearbook "Talon," receive recognition as excellent publications.

- Edison has a National Merit Scholarship Finalist as well as commended students.

(Honor roll, Attendance, and Miscellaneous data are reported in the original report.)

Phase III (1996-97)

In Phase III of the T. A. Edison High School Restructured School Day schedule, the semester/semester plan will continue to be implemented and strengthened. Attention will continue to be given to areas of concern including the following:

- Balancing of students' academic workload between terms.

- Appropriate sequencing of courses.

- Scheduling of AP course options to maximize students' learning and to enhance performance on AP exams.

- Paring of embedded course options.

- Staff Development

- Curriculum development aimed at enhancement of student performance particularly in the area of math.

- Minimizing the number of scheduling changes by implementing a strengthened multi-step registration process.

- New courses have been added to include:
  -Geoscience
  -Technical Theater
  -Principles of Technology
  -AP Government with Seminar (year long option)
  -Introduction to the Hotel Industry
  -AP Seminar Interdisciplinary

-Algebra I (year long)

For next year, a forty-five hour course designed to improve instruction during the 90-minute block schedule will be offered on-site to a core of Edison faculty. The course content will be designed to meet the unique needs of Edison's staff and will be based on a faculty survey conducted during Spring, 1996.

The student course registration process has been improved to afford students more guidance in selecting courses for the Phase III year. Beginning in January and running through March, scheduling for the 1996-97 school year will be done through a comprehensive five step process involving students, parents, teachers, and counselors. In addition, electives will be advertised through an electives fair.

Edison High School as an Instructional Leader

The Edison Model has been the subject of much study by other schools and experts in school restructuring. The Edison Model has become the premiere model that avoids some of the pitfalls of purely alternating-day models such as those at many other Fairfax County High Schools. Inquiries, visitations, and expert citations include:

* References to the success of the Edison Model by Dr. Lynn Canady in his video on school restructuring

* Inquiries and visitations from the following schools and regions include:

-Rochester, NY	-Lamorre, CA
-N. Stafford H.S., VA	-T.C. Williams H.S., VA
-Coral Shores H.S., FL	-Rancocas Valley H.S., NJ
-Dartmouth H.S., MA	-Chantilly H.S., VA
-James Madison H.S., NJ	-Western H.S., KY
-Rush Henrietta H.S., NY	-Stetson University, FL
-Roosevelt H.S., OH	-McDonough H.S., MD
-Falls Church H.S., VA	-Waysato Sr. H.S., MN
-Lexington, SC	-Branford, CT
-Masuk H.S., CT	-Verona H.S., WI
-Hoover H.S., AL	-Lee H.S., VA
-Fauquier H.S., VA	-Monroe H.S., VA

The following description has been provided by Luther W. Fennell, Principal, regarding the music offerings and embedded courses at Thomas A. Edison High School.

Embedded Courses and Music Offerings

"In response to concerns articulated by band students, their parents, and the band director as to the limitations associated with a pure semester/semester block scheduling model, it was determined that the music program at Thomas A. Edison High School would benefit by being scheduled on an alternating day basis.

In arranging the program in this manner it was possible for band students to remain in band for an entire year and to also be able to participate for credit each of their four years in high school. It provided the necessary instructional support for the marching band season and provided continuity as to the programs associated with band such as, festivals, competitions and concerts. Overall, this arrangement has worked well. Enrollments have held and in some instances they have increased. The quality of our marching band program has continued to be strengthened, and the performance levels have remained strong. We believe the "embedded alternating day model" is a positive and substantive response to the legitimate concerns as raised by the various stake holder groups."

Sample Student Schedule With
Four *Embedded* Courses
Which Meet Every Other Day

First Term		Second Term	
AP Government	AP English	AP Government	AP English
Physics 1		Spanish 5	
Photo-journalism	Advanced Band Level 4	Photo-journalism	Advanced Band Level 4
Math Analysis		Human Anatomy	

Sample Student Schedule With
Two *Embedded* Courses
Which Meet Every Other Day

First Term		Second Term	
Advanced Symphonic Strings	Theater Arts	Advanced Symphonic Strings	Theater Arts
Geometry		English	
HPE 10		German I	
Biology 1		Army ROTC	

BLOCK 8 - EIGHT PERIODS
ROTATING A B DAYS

This form of block scheduling is used at Carmel High School in Indianapolis, Indiana - home of one of the premier comprehensive music education programs in the United States. The descriptions that follow have been provided by Mr. Ronald D. Hellems, Chairman of the Performing Arts Department and are used with permission.

The following is a brief summary of Carmel High School's Block Eight Schedule, and its effect on the Performing Arts Department. Carmel High School has made a minimum <u>Three Year</u> commitment to the plan. In addition, the 1995-96 school year brought about other major adjustments and situations that we were called upon to deal with at the same time: primarily, moving ninth graders to our school for the first time (increasing enrollment significantly, causing need for major curriculum additions and revisions, and presenting our staff with entirely new teaching scenarios), and the planning and beginning of a major school renovation project (causing restrictions on facilities, parking, etc.). We did indeed have a full plate!

The Block Eight Schedule was implemented at the beginning of the 1995-96 school year, after much discussion, debate, etc. We, of the Performing Arts

Department, were strongly against this type of schedule, and were extremely verbal about our displeasure in all the debates. The members of our Foreign Language Department were also against the plan, but chose to remain relatively silent throughout the debate sessions. The remainder of the CHS faculty were generally favorable to this plan, and it passed by approximately a 75% vote of the entire faculty.

I should note, that once the decision was officially made, the Performing Arts Department made no further negative opinions about the plan to any other staff member, administrator, or community patron. We (the PAD Staff) were of the definite feeling that our verbal and aggressive disapproval of the Block Eight plan had caused a great deal of hard feelings among our faculty. We felt that it would be important to "squelch" those feelings immediately, and set about to jump on the "bandwagon" and turn the negatives into positives. Today, one year later, I believe we made a mistake by opposing the change so adamantly, and would encourage other Performing Arts educators to channel their energies in other directions. All energy and emotions should be directed at continuing their pursuits for performance excellence.

Advantages of the Block 8

• Longer rehearsal sessions prove to be positive.

• By scheduling certain performing groups during the "lunch block" each day (Periods 3 & 7), we are able to complete field trips/performances for community luncheons, etc. during the group's own class period only--thus keeping students from missing other "academic" classes (And keeping "academic" staff VERY HAPPY!!!)

• Enrollment in all "elective" classes soared, as a result of the requirement for students to enroll in seven periods (no study halls).

• The SRT (Student Resource Time) period does offer opportunities for small group, or large ensemble rehearsals when needed.

Disadvantages of the Block 8

• By meeting ensembles every other day, organizational procedures are difficult to maintain, especially at concert or performance time, making certain that all your groups get the same information.

• "Follow-up" and consistency are difficult when meeting every other day (i.e., musical concepts, discipline, organization, etc.).

• Students have a three-day weekend instead of a two-day weekend from every subject - A long gap between rehearsals!

• SRT (Student Resource Time) needs to be very well planned and executed, or it becomes WST (Wasted

Student Time), or AIT (Administrative Interruption Time).

After one year, I can honestly say that we feel there has been NO destructive or negative impact on the Performing Arts Program as a result of switching to the Block Eight Schedule.   It certainly has required adjustment on everyone's part, and my personal feelings about all aspects of the program are not completely positive.   However, I believe that any Performing Arts Program that strives for, and expects excellence from its staff and students will be able to achieve their desired goals no matter how their daily schedule is designed. We feel that with very little effort, we have successfully made the switch to the Block Eight Schedule, simply by doing our jobs, and remaining focused on performing arts objectives. We do intend to follow the progression of our students during the coming years, and to evaluate their musical skills on a regular basis, in order to better determine the "long-term" effects of the scheduling change on our program.

The chart that follows outlines the period options of the Block 8.   Please note the time schedule with the four variations to accommodate the daily lunch periods. An activity/conference period is also scheduled as an extension of the regularly scheduled day.

Block 8 - Alternating Day Bell Schedule

Blue Day	Gold Day	Time
Period 1	Period 5	7:50-9:20
Period 2	Period 6 (Homeroom) & SRT	9:30-11:03 (Announcements
Period 3	Period 7	**A** 11:03-11:38 Lunch 11:46- 1:23 Class **B** 11:13-11:41 Class 11:46-12:13 Lunch 12:21- 1:23 Class **C** 11:13-12:16 Class 12:21-12:48 Lunch 12:56- 1:23 Class **D** 11:13-12:48 Class 12:56- 1:23 Lunch
Period 4	Period 8	1:33-3:05 (Announcements)
Activity Period - Conference		3:10-3:25

The following presents the overall CHS schedule indicating the unique SRT which provides special opportunities for music students, home room with Sustained Silent Reading (SSR) and Student Resource Time (SRT).

CHS Block 8 Master Schedule, 1995-96

Blue Mon.	*Gold* Tues.	*Blue* Wed.	*Gold* Thur.	*Blue* Fri.	*Blue* Mon.	*Gold* Tues.	*Blue* Wed.	*Gold* Thur.	*Blue* Fri.
1	5	1	5	1	5	1	5	1	5
2	HR-1 SRT-1	2	HR-1 SRT-2	2	HR-1 SRT-1	2	HR-1 SRT-2	2	HR-1 SRT-3
3	6	3	6	3	6	3	6	3	6
4	7	4	7	4	7	4	7	4	7

HR-1	30 minutes for SSR (Sustained Silent Reading) and announcements
SRT-1	63 minutes for passing and student resource time
HR-2,3	15 minutes for announcements and administrivia
SRT-2,3	78 minutes for passing, student resource time, convocations, meetings, etc.

Goals of the Block 8 Schedule
Carmel High School

- Provide a wider variety of learning experiences for students

- Provide greater instructional flexibility for the classroom teacher

- Increase student and faculty attendance

- Reduce the number of student disciplinary referrals

- Reduce the stress level of both students and staff

Carmel High School Administration
Dr. R. Stephen Tegarden, Superintendent of Schools
Dr. William Duke, Principal Carmel High School
Mr. Eric Clard, Assistant Principal
Mr. T. J. White, Assistant Principal
Mr. John Abell, Administrative Assistant
Mr. Robert Grenda, Administrative Assistant
Ms. Denise Jacobs, Administrative Assistant
Mr. Jeff Lazo, Administrative Assistant
Mr. Lee Lonzo, Athletic Director
Mr. Bruce Wolf, Assistant Athletic Director

Performing Arts Department Staff
Mrs. Ann C. Conrad, Director of Vocal Music
Mr. Thomas O. Dick, Director of Orchestra
Mr. Ronald D. Hellems, Director of Vocal Music
Department Chairman
Mr. Kenneth H. Knowles, Assistant
Auditorium Director
Mr. Paul Bernard Killian, Auditorium Director
Mr. Christopher Kreke, Associate Band Director
Mr. James Peterson, Director of Drama
Mr. Michael Pote, Associate Director of Bands
Mr. Richard L. Saucedo, Director of Bands
Mrs. Rebecca Sendi, String Assistant
Miss Tamara Tudor, Director of Drama

MODIFIED BLOCK SCHEDULING
"SPLIT BLOCK" CLASSES

The following description of the "Split Block" scheduling option is contributed by Mr. Chuck Edwards, Director of Bands at Bourbon County High School in Paris, Kentucky. Presented is the process of planning and working with the administration and faculty to achieve this option. The descriptive narrative follows.

The Planning Process

During the 1995-96 school year, Bourbon County High School began block scheduling but with a unique option for some of the students. Like most four period block scheduling models in Kentucky, most of the students day is divided into four blocks of 90 minutes. During each block a student at Bourbon County High School may take one class that for the entire semester or they may choose to take two classes which last for nine weeks each. In addition, the Bourbon County schedule allows students to have the option during a primary block (90 minutes) to choose two 45 minute classes rather than the one 90 minute class. These divided block classes are referred to as "split block" classes. Approximately thirty to forty percent of the Bourbon County students choose this option. Below is a list of the 45 minute classes that are available during the "split block."

Split Block Class Options

Class	Credit	Class	Credit
Agriculture I	1.0	Flags	0.5
Agriscience II	0.5	Gifted-Talented*	1.0
Animal Science	0.5	Integ. Social Science*	1.0
Aquaculture	0.5	Journalism II-IV	1.0
Band	1.0	Keyboard Applications*	0.5
Choir	1.0	Parent Education*	0.5
Computer Key*	0.5	Peer Tutoring*	0.5-1
Contemp. Issues*	0.5	Spanish I*	1.0
Driver's Ed.*	0.5	US History*	1.0
Explor. Tech.*	0.5-1	Vegetable Gardening	0.5
Life Skills*	0.5	World Civilization*	1.0

*These classes are also available during a 90 minute block.

Daily Schedule

Whole Block Option   *Split Block Option*

Block One	Block One
Block Two	Block Two
Block Three	Split Block One
	Lunch
Lunch	Split Block Two
Block Four	Block Four

About Bourbon County High School

By Kentucky standards, Bourbon County High School is a medium sized high school with a student population of approximately 750. The school has one principle, two assistant principals, two guidance counselors and a faculty of approximately fifty. The current principal is beginning his second year at BCHS and the music director is beginning his seventh year. The school district is generally rural with horse farming being the largest employer; however, the county is close to Lexington, Kentucky - the state's second largest city and Georgetown, Kentucky - home of a large Toyota automotive plant. Most of Bourbon County's residents live within a thirty minute commute to work.

The Bourbon County Music Program

The music program at BCHS includes classes in band and choir. High school band enrollment has not varied much over the past five years. However, due to some personnel changes and additional administrative support, band enrollment is up drastically at the middle school. These changes have begun to affect the size and quality of the high school band program. Because of a larger than normal freshman band class, this years high school band enrollment has increased over recent years. Considering the relatively small size of the current junior and senior band classes and the expected growth of future freshman band classes, an increase in band enrollment is expected over the next five years.

The choir enrollment has grown steadily over the past five years and peaked last year due to a number of senior band members needing an additional "split block" class and currently has decreased due to a change in the way freshman are scheduled (unrelated to block scheduling). The music department is currently working on some changes which may help keep freshman in the program. If these solutions are not effective, declining enrollment will be the trend.

The Planning Process for Block Scheduling at BCHS

During the spring semester of 1993, a committee was

formed to discuss implementing block scheduling - possibly for the next school year. The music director served on this committee and was successful with persuading the committee to delay any drastic scheduling changes for the next school year. Later that summer another committee was formed to study block scheduling. The music director volunteered to serve but was not selected. The following fall during professional development training, block scheduling was discussed and it was decided that a straight four block plan would be adopted for the next school year.

In an attempt to become more informed about the ramifications and potential consequences of going to block scheduling, the music director set out to gather material and research on the effects of Block Scheduling and Performing Arts Classes. Information was gathered from the Morehead State University Department of Music, the University of Kentucky Library, E.R.I.C., and other sources.

Findings were presented to the principal, the curriculum committee and the site based council members. Fortunately, the principal and several site-based members were supportive and expressed the need for more information and facts concerning the potential damaging effects on the music program.

A group of allies began to surface. As mentioned earlier, Bourbon county's largest employer is the horse industry. Due to this local economic interest, the agriculture department at BCHS is unusually large and particularly good. All four of the agriculture faculty members joined the team to express concern over choosing the appropriate form of scheduling to fit the needs of our school.

After much deliberation, an alternative form of scheduling from the full block option was proposed - the "split block" option. This form seemed to be a more reasonable alternative for the school and was adopted.

With the addition of the split block, block scheduling has not had any major effect on the instrumental music program, but has had some adverse effects on the vocal program. The biggest complaint from students addressed the need to have a larger variety of classes offered in the split. The expected growth of the band could further complicate scheduling concerns, or it may contribute to its' solution depending on how the faculty and administration decide to handle the potential needs.

The success of block scheduling at BCHS must be attributed the outstanding leadership of the principals. Most important has been the adherence to the idea that *all stake holders should have a voice in decisions and their tolerance for differing points of view.* This approach has been crucial to the success of restructuring the scheduling at BCHS.

It has been said that managers do things right,
but leaders do the right thing.

THE INTENSIVE BLOCK FIVE

The Intensive Block Five is utilized at Upper Darby High School in Philadelphia. This form of block scheduling includes a school-wide split block to allow for lunch and singleton classes (38 minute periods). The following presentation of this creative approach to scheduling is provided by G. Scott Litzenberg, Instrumental Director at Upper Darby High School.

The Upper Darby *Intensive* (Block) Experiment

Upper Darby High School is located on the West border with the City of Philadelphia. We are a small area with a very high concentration of residential dwellings (210 square miles and 95,000 people). Our district has approximately 11,000 students with 3,200 enrolled in the high school. We have a very diverse ethnic population that covers approximately 35 different languages spoken in our district.

Our experiment with intensive scheduling began two and a half years ago during a faculty meeting that featured the principal from Hatboro Horsham High School. The usual questions from the faculty were then followed by a scary statement from the visiting principal. He said, "This system has worked great for our whole program in all areas except one, MUSIC." My colleague and I both looked at each other with genuine concern.

The intensive schedule was not the only beast that we were dealing with during the last two and a half years. We started a major 21 million dollar renovation and addition project to our building from 1994 to 1995. This was a result of increased enrollment. March of 1995 was our Middle States Review, and we changed principals in January of 1995 because of a retirement. Needless to say, it has been very hectic at Upper Darby High School over the last two years!

With an enrollment of approximately 3,000 students, we are fortunate at Upper Darby High School to be supported very strongly in the area of music and the other arts. We have the following scheduled music classes offered during the school day: Chorus, Choir, Encore Singers (a small select choir), String Orchestra, Wind Ensemble, Concert Band, two Jazz Ensembles, and Piano Class. If the principal at Hatboro Horsham High School had difficulty fitting in their music classes, how were we going to fit into this system the number of ensembles that we offer? We were nervous to say the least.

The Planning Process and
Concerns With Scheduling Music Classes

One of our first concerns was how will courses that perform for a whole year fit into a semester concept. Little did we know that our school size would be an asset in scheduling our courses for an entire year. Our Assistant Principal in charge of the massive scheduling for our school was very creative and supportive of our needs in enabling us to actually improve our programs as a result of this intensive scheduling.

On our earlier schedule, our students had been allowed to waive their lunch in order to fit in extra courses such as band and choir. This was needed by the Honors and AP students who were trying to develop their courses of study to prepare for the top universities that all of our honors students wish to gain acceptance to. Many of our top musicians took 4-5 Honors/AP courses plus their minor electives. As a result of the lunch waiver, last year, out of 54 students in my Wind Ensemble, 49 of them ate lunch for the first 10-15 minutes of the 46 minute class. It was hard to start rehearsal and get very much ensemble time each day. This year, I have 4-5 students eating lunch during the class. With our 39 minute 1/2 block, I can start when needed and have actually gained rehearsal time over last years longer period.

Because of the size of our school, it was decided that we would have to utilize five blocks instead of four in order to have four 750 student lunch periods. One thousand-five-hundred students per lunch was just not feasible with the four block system. Since every student was scheduled to have 1/2 of a block for lunch, we thought that our ensembles which needed to meet for a whole year would be perfect to fit in the outer half of the lunch block. One of the main roadblocks to this concept was that many departments were also pulling at these 1/2 blocks for other potential course offerings.

We have a very extensive Advanced Placement (AP) program at Upper Darby High School. The AP teachers had a legitimate concern that if a student had the AP course in the fall semester, they would have 3-4 months between the end of the class and the date of the AP test. They wanted to use the 1/2 block that the students would have opposite their lunch for a semester seminar to review and continue the AP material (until the testing companies catch-up with this new concept, this will continue to be a concern). My colleague and I both realized that many of our kids were the same students who were in the AP programs and would be affected by this move. The move to the five block system actually helped to minimize the AP problem unless the AP seminar was offered at the same time as the ensemble that the student was assigned to (you can not avoid every conflict in any system). As a result of going to five blocks, the students had room for ten blocks a year as compared to eight periods in our old scheduling system. I don't think we could have kept our program intact with a four block system.

Upper Darby High School
Former Traditional Schedule for Music

46 minute periods	Instrumental	Vocal
period 1	Jazz-A(MTR) B(TF)	Chorus
period 2	Orchestra - WRF	Encore Singers - WRF
period 3	Duty	Choir
period 4	Lunch	
period 5	Concert Band	
period 6	Wind Ensemble	
period 7	Piano Class	
period 8	Prep	

Upper Darby High School
New Intensive Block Schedule for Music Classes

	Instrumental	Vocal
Block 1 80 minutes	Semester 1 - Piano Class Semester 2 - Piano Class	*
Block 2 80 minutes	Semester 1 - Jazz Fund. Semester 2 - Jazz Band	*half block* - * *half block* - Duty
Block 3 38 minute periods	*half block* - Lunch *half block* - Orchestra	Choir Encore Singers
Block 4 38 minute periods	*half block* - Wind Ensemble *half block* - Concert Band	Chorus
Block 5 80 minutes	Prep	Lunch/Prep

* District Music Supervisor teaches 1/2 schedule

How We Made Block Scheduling Work

One of our biggest concerns was losing courses that we currently offered as a result of the scheduling. We prioritized our courses and tried to figure out which ensembles might involve the same students so that conflicts within our department would be minimal. Usually, if a student is one of my top instrumental students and in the vocal program, he/she is also one of the top vocal students. We tried to not schedule our top ensembles together so these students would be less affected. Also, I thought very hard about our two jazz bands that we offered.

Since we had both advanced and beginning jazz ensembles at Upper Darby, I began to realize that most of our Jazz performances are spring festivals, trips, and concerts for jazz, and that we should have the beginning ensemble in the fall and the advanced group in the spring. This involved into a changing the beginning ensemble into a Jazz Fundamentals course. During the 82 minute period, students work in small combos, learn jazz theory and fundamentals, explore the history of jazz, and gain individual help on jazz techniques. What a bonus! The fall semester of jazz fundamentals was wonderful! The hardest part was writing curriculum and needing different materials than what was used for the beginning ensemble in the past. One additional plus was that some of the advanced jazz students were able to roster this course in addition to the Jazz Ensemble in order to hone their skills. That was not possible in the past.

My biggest concern about the Advanced Jazz Ensemble, was only having four to five weeks to prepare for our first jazz festival and concerts. Our first performance on March 2nd was subsequently fine. We have been able to do so much more with the 82 minute block five days a week than was accomplished during three days a week, 45 minutes a day in the old system. Better warm-ups, sectional time, individual practice time, listening, ensemble time, and the building of endurance have all be a plus.

We previously offered a piano class for one semester, two days a week - a total of 90 minutes a week with five days between classes. Retention was not one of the students' strong points in that class. We had been recommended by our last Middle States Review to add a theory program at Upper Darby but were unable to add it to our curriculum. With this new system, our piano class was expanded to a Piano/Theory class that now meets one semester, five days a week for a full 82 minute block. What a difference! I have students finishing the second book of our method along with learning theory at a much more adequate and involved level. What a treat to teach and to see the students getting so much out of this part of our program. We are already anticipating a major increase with the enrollment.

The Impact of the Intensive Block Scheduling On the Music Program

Overall, our program has surprisingly seen a great improvement as a result of this new schedule. We have had fewer scheduling conflicts than in the past, our actual rehearsal time has improved, our use of facilities has improved, and the attitude of the students towards this has been super. We are hoping to increase our department faculty size from two in the future.

I can not say enough about the support from our principal and others to help us make this transition a very positive one for our program and students at Upper Darby. I hope you can make this work as well and that you will be as flexible and as creative as you can. Who knows, maybe even your program has room for improvement. I am glad that ours did!

BLOCK 4 SCHEDULING WITH AN EXTENDED DAY OPTION

The following schedule type involves a split block with an extension of the school day option for music and physical education classes. An overview of this type of scheduling with the goals, implementation procedures and impact on the music program is presented. This description has been submitted by Rick Whitcomb, Band Director at Haverford Senior High School in Havertown, Pennsylvania.

Overview

When we were informed that block scheduling was coming to Haverford, we immediately knew that if we stood on the sidelines and let others determine the future of music scheduling, that future might be indeed be bleak. Our best defense was to get in the game and develop a list of priorities and proposals to address our needs.

The Haverford Township School District, with a high school population of approximately 1,500 students, has an active music program with instrumental groups including a concert band, wind ensemble and orchestra, and choral groups consisting of the concert chorale and chamber singers which meet as a part of the scheduled student day. Haverford also has a successful jazz band which meets outside the standard school day.

A standard student school day is structured as four 85 minute blocks and and a 30 minute lunch period, with six minutes passing time between each block. Music rehearsals are scheduled during the final 85 minute session, which has come to be named Block 4a and 4b.   An additional 45 minute period is an important part of the music students' schedule, as sectional rehearsals for all music ensemble members and physical education classes for some are scheduled at this time, depending on the configuration of the student's academic schedule. This extension of the school day is utilized only by those students who are either in music, or need their gym classes at the end of the day for a variety of scheduling circumstances. The vast majority of the general student population is dismissed prior to this extended time.

The Goals

During the planning stages for our first year of block scheduling last spring, our highest priorities as a music department were to preserve the quality of instruction and contact time with our ensembles, and configure a schedule which would allow our students to continue to participate in multiple music ensembles, as many of them had under the previous traditional seven period day. The choral director, orchestra director, department chairman and I were also in agreement that it was imperative that students be enrolled in the ensembles for the entire year to prevent the obvious catastrophic results of changing personnel and instrumentation each semester.

Implementation

We determined that our best chance to achieve our goals was to devise a format where as many of our major performance ensembles as possible would meet within the same time period. We were also able to structure our groups so that the ensembles would meet for the entire school year by splitting the 85 minute block into two 40 minute periods (4a & 4b) with a five minute passing time between. We set the format with the advanced vocal and instrumental ensembles meeting on opposite sides of the block, so that our students who have participated in both vocal and instrumental music would have the best chance of continuing this practice. In this scenario, students could elect two music ensembles, participate in both for the whole school year, still have six other blocks available for other courses, and take their required physical education courses in a specially scheduled time slot at the end of the normal school day. Students not electing six courses other than music take their gym classes within the normal school schedule. Another, less preferable, option which a very few students needed was to schedule their physical education classes during either Block 4a or 4b two days a week for one semester and attend their ensemble rehearsals on the other three days. The remaining semester was left intact. This was necessary if the students could not be placed into an after school gym class due to their extensive involvement in multiple music sectionals.

One of the strengths of our music program in the past has been our ability to creatively share students between our ensemble rehearsals. Traditionally, selected players from the band have attended orchestra rehearsal once a week to practice with the strings. We were able to continue to offer a full orchestra experience to our students by scheduling the wind ensemble and the advanced string group, listed as String Ensemble in the following illustration, during the "half block." For those students who are selected for vocal and instrumental ensembles which meet during the same portion of the block, the students alternate days between the two groups.

For those students who are members of only one performing group, we, in a cooperative effort with the guidance department and administration, have devised a way for the music students to maximize their time and avoid study halls in the opposing half block. Required half-credit courses such as a senior thesis course, Health, Public Speaking and the aforementioned Physical Education have been scheduled in both 4a and 4b exclusively for music students. Additionally, two half-credit English courses, Creative Writing and Shakespeare have served to address the academic needs of our upperclassmen.

The following presents the Block 4 Format for the music classes in both semester one and two along with the (*extended*) end of the day sectionals.

Block 4 Format for Music Classes

	SEMESTER 1		SEMESTER 2
Block 4A (40 minutes) **Passing Time** (5 minutes)	Wind Ensemble *	String Ensemble *	Concert Chorale
Block 4B (40 minutes)	Concert Band	String Orchestra	Chamber Singers *

End of Day Sectionals

Monday	Tuesday	Wednesday	Thursday	Friday
Orchestra Winds Chorale Men	Combined Band Strings Chambers Men	Chorale Women	Jazz Band Chambers Women	Percussion Choral Make Up

Conclusion

As can be seen from the above description, achieving our goals within the confines of block scheduling has not been an easy task. The ultimate key to our success and survival has been our willingness to get involved in the process. The accommodations outlined above were achieved through numerous brainstorming sessions and meetings, both amongst our music staff and with building administrators. We realize that more is needed to even better serve our students, but we agree that this is a positive approach to the block scheduling issue.

So far the disadvantage of moving to block scheduling has only been the addition of more paperwork. The major advantage has been a marked increase in the number of band members and more contact time per student.

The following suggestion is for those music teachers having to deal with moving to block scheduling. Even if you reach a viable solution to the block scheduling scenario, stay informed and *in the loop*. It is a short jump from either half-block year-long scheduling which we have, or true one course per semester block scheduling, to finding your rehearsals outside the instructional school day.

BLOCK 8 - 7 CREDIT SCHEDULE
ROTATING DAYS
WITH ALL 8 CLASSES MEETING ON FRIDAY

The following schedule represents an additional option for those considering a modified type of block scheduling. Unlike other forms of Block 8 scheduling which rotate 4 classes every other day, this plan allows for a 4 block rotation along with one day in which all classes meet. This description has been submitted by Gary McCarty, Band Director, at Emporia High School, in Emporia, Kansas.

Overview

The following information is based on Gary McCarty's description and also contains excerpts from the Emporia High School manual on block scheduling: *The Spartan 8 Block / 7 Credit Schedule,* Emporia High School, 3302 West 18th Street, Emporia, Kansas.

Emporia High School is located in East-central Kansas, on I - 35, halfway between Wichita and Kansas City. EHS is a 6A school with approximately 1,400 students in grades 9-12. The school has a predominantly white student body, with a large number of Hispanic and Asiatic students.

We were on a traditional 6-period schedule, and were under pressure from a small, but vocal, group of parents who wanted us to add a seventh class, which would allow the students more electives. The mandate came from our Board of Education to change to a seven-credit schedule, but we were allowed to implement it the way we wanted. After studying and visiting several schools (approximately one-half year), we (the staff) chose a variation of the 8-block schedule we had seen at Hillcrest High School in Springfield, Missouri.

The next year and a half was spent in committee work to design the schedule to fit our needs and situation. Considerable effort was spent on the Seminar, which we felt would be the key to the program. During this time, we also held several In-services on the schedule itself, and on teaching the 90-minute block of time. Finally, in 1994, after two full years of development, we began our present schedule.

The following extracts are from the EHS school manual: *The Spartan 8 Block / 7 Credit Schedule.*

Emporia High School 8 Block Schedule

Emporia High School has adopted a modified 8 Block schedule. Until the 1993-94 school year students were scheduled into a six-period day with 55 to 60 minute classes. During the 1993-94 school year several zero hour courses were offered.

The Emporia schedule is a block schedule of

seven 90 minute classes which takes two days to complete. On Tuesday-Thursday the second block period of the day is a non-credit (grade does not count for credit) seminar period in which enrichment and remediation activities are offered for all students. This allows each student at least 180 minutes per week of teacher assisted study time. Seminar consists of approximately 20 students total from 9 through 12. This period is highly structured for students and is to be used for academic related activities.

On Fridays closure is reached by having all seven classes meet for 42 minutes. The academic seminar is shortened to 35 minutes and provides the opportunity for organization meetings to be held. Friday seminar is scheduled during the next-to-the-last block of the day. This allows seminar to be moved to the last block by switching with Block 7 when necessary (such as when a pep rally is scheduled).

During the seminar period, students report to their assigned seminar rooms for attendance. The student may remain in that room as a study period or may sign out to any other teacher in the building. Students who need additional time with another teacher will have the option of spending the period with that teacher for additional help. The student will carry their seminar pass with them any time they leave the seminar room. Hall monitors (assigned faculty) check the passes to be sure the students are moving along and headed in the right direction. Students are expected to return to their seminar room five minutes before the end of the seminar period. In effect, every student has a directed study period every other day.

There are many interruptions of the educational process in a high school. Required testing, student council meetings, assemblies, etc. take time away from the students time-on-task. With few exceptions, those interruptions take place during the seminar period.

Advantages of the 8 Block Schedule

a.   Research by American College Test (ACT) provides clear evidence that students who take the recommended college preparatory courses in English, mathematics, science, and social studies score better on the ACT than students who do not take those courses. The 8 Block/seven credit schedule provides an increased opportunity for students to schedule the classes that they consider important.

b.   By meeting classes every other day, students have more time to organize and prepare for their classes.

c.   We consider fine arts and practical arts to be important areas of study. An increase in the number of credit opportunities for students should increase enrollment in fine arts and practical arts classes.

d.   Students have two evenings in which to complete their homework.

e.   Students have only four classes to prepare for each day.

f.   Less time is lost in moving from one class to another.

g.   There are fewer opportunities to be tardy.

h.   The longer class periods require creativity from the teacher.

i.   The longer class periods provide the opportunity for the teacher to accommodate a variety of learning styles.

j.   The additional credit opportunity supports student athletes.

k.   A greater diversity of activities are possible in a longer period:
    * guest speakers
    * more complex laboratory experiments
    * field trips
    * better use of audio-visual resources

An example of the weekly 8 Block - 7 Credit Time Schedule follows.

Emporia High School
8 Block - 7 Credit Time Schedule

Time	Mon	Tues	Wed	Thurs	Fri	Time
8:00 - 9:30	2	1	2	1	1	8:00 - 8:42
					2	8:47 - 9:29
9:35 - 11:05	4	3	4	3	Seminar	9:34- 10:09
		Seminar		Seminar	4	10:14- 10:56
11:10- 1:12	6	5	6	5	5	11:01- 11:43
	Lunch	Lunch	Lunch	Lunch	6 - Lunch	11:48- 1:13
1:17 - 2:47	8	7	8	7	7	1:18- 2:00
					8	2:05- 2:47

Advantages and Disadvantages Experienced With Block Scheduling

Disadvantages
• We don't see the music students every day.

• Not seeing students every day affects the program scheduling. Concerts should be scheduled on rehearsal days. Such things as announcements have to be planned very carefully.

Advantages
- Both students and teachers learn to plan and organize time.

- Students have more time (Seminar) to do homework. They are taking less homework home, and we are getting more homework turned in.

- Students have more responsibility for their own education.

- Teachers have a 90-minute preparation period every day (each still teaches 5 classes, plus Seminar). Teachers are taking less work home.

- Students have more time to prepare assignments; they get an assignment on Monday that is due on Wednesday.

- Recruiter visits and standardized tests, etc., are only allowed during Seminar. Classes are not interrupted.

- There is LESS STRESS.

- There is more time for rehearsals.

Suggestions for Music Teachers Dealing With Block Scheduling

- Be PRO-active! Get involved in the planning process.

- Develop a schedule that works for YOUR music department. Do this quickly. Be FIRST IN LINE.

- Develop and maintain a positive outlook on the schedule. What can you do to make it to your advantage?

- Develop a means of planning rehearsals carefully; perhaps develop a form to use which will help you stay organized.

Conclusion

We like the current block schedule because on Fridays we see every class. We meet with each class three times a week, as opposed to the "alternate days" schedule. As schools plan for the change to block scheduling, be aware that there are many different forms of "The Block." For instance, we believe that the "4-Block" is the death of music programs. Every school must invent the schedule which will work for them.

CHAPTER 4

Making Block Scheduling Work
One Program at a Time

Our work with block scheduling has put us in direct contact with many exceptional music education professionals. One of these special people is Gail Crum, Information Services Manager for MENC. A primary goal of our work from the beginning has been to provide music teachers with information for informed decision-making about block scheduling - **useful** information compiled by music teachers for music teachers. At the beginning of September of this year, we made yet another call to Gail to check the "status" of the block scheduling issue on a national level. She indicated that block scheduling was still the number one topic that music educators across the country were questioning this year. Gail stated that in a recent State Leadership Update, she had sent the following "plea" for information: "As part of our ongoing effort to provide helpful information to music teachers faced with concerns about block scheduling, MENC is looking for examples of 'what works' for music programs. Please send the names and addresses of schools in your state where music programs have been unaffected by, or have benefited from, block scheduling." The "what

works for music programs" concept seemed to be in line
with our own efforts, and we decide to once again join
forces.   Within a few days, Gail had faxed us her list of
schools and addresses identified by the State
Leadership Update.   We were able to put specific
names with 25 of these schools from 13 states, and in
mid-September we sent out our own plea for
information to these 25 teachers who were "making it
work." Now while mid-September may not be the best
time to ask for information from busy music teachers,
many of whom had just stated a new school year, we
knew from personal experience that music teachers are
always busy, and generally make time to share
information with colleagues when possible.   We did,
however, made a decision not to "remind" any of these
teachers with follow-up requests, and by the end of
September, we had received 15 responses.   The
information received from teachers in three of these
schools is included in Chapter 4.   Additionally, we made
a decision to include schools reporting high school
schedule information.   One person responded by phone
almost immediately, thanking us for our efforts, and
indicating that he was enjoying his recent retirement.
He had, however, already forwarded our request to
another teacher for a response (music teachers are
caring folks).

The questionnaire used to gather information

was designed with one straight-forward purpose: to give music teachers a chance to tell other music teachers what they needed to know when dealing with block scheduling. We included a cover letter and a one-page guide that asked teachers to provide:

1. a brief description of their school and location;
2. the type of schedule that they were currently using;
3. a brief description of the process they went through to get their current schedule;
4. advantages/disadvantages experienced using block scheduling; and,
5. specific suggestions for music teachers dealing with block scheduling

We also requested a little bit of demographic information, encouraged the music teachers to share information in a way that was best for them, and suggested that they include any additional information they wished. The responses from the teachers in the 10 remaining schools follow.

Name: Alida W. Menefee
Position: Choral Director
School: Coatesville Area Intermediate School
              Coatesville, Pennsylvania

1. School Description:

* located approximately 4 miles west of Philadelphia
* approximately 1000 students, 9th and 10th grade only
* 2 full-time choral directors (9-10, 11-12)
* 1 full-time band director
(band combined 9-12)
* 1 orchestra teacher who also services all 3 middle schools

2. Schedule Description:

* 6-day cycle, 4 periods per day
* chorus scheduled on opposite days from band/ orchestra (scheduled together) so students can do both; example:
    Chorus (period 4) on days 1,3,5
    Band/Orchestra (period 4) on days 2,4,6

3. Development of Current Schedule:

* not much in-service, we were told research shows that it doesn't make any difference if you have training or not
* met with Assistant Superintendent and planned our schedules, 4th period every day was "Music Block" for band/orchestra, and most selective chorus offerings, certain periods were designated "language, honors, etc."

4. Advantages/Disadvantages:

• some courses had to be dropped from the course selection guide because of lack of time in our schedules and no additional staff
• concentrated time helps rehearsal, kids know music better
• gives me more time to do stuff I hadn't been able to do well, like listening to selections in class, more sightreading time

5. Specific suggestions:

• be sure to get a "music block" that works <u>really well</u> for you
• don't panic

6. Additional Information:

• be prepared to have to drop stuff or get <u>new</u> <u>staff</u> (fat chance!)

Name: Bill Gibson
Position: Music Director
School: Kingswood Regional High School
          Wolfeboro, New Hampshire

1. School Description:

It is an 800 student 9-12 high school in the "Lakes Region" of New Hampshire. We are a regional school with students from six different communities with a

320 square mile radius.

2. Schedule Description:

We are on a 4x4 block with 4 classes per semester, each 90 minutes in length. However, the music classes, band and chorus, which run year-long, are 45 minutes in length during the 2nd block of the day. There are 4 other classes which run against this all year long, plus a study hall.

3. Development of Current Schedule

We studied block scheduling for a year looking at neighboring schools in Maine. We also used the Internet for information from the Western schools that had tried block scheduling. I had to fight and scrap to keep the performing ensembles as a year long course with only 1 credit, so people here sometimes think that music runs the schedule which in a way it has to. This is our second year and we made one change - from band and chorus 90 minutes every other day to the present - 45 minutes every day.

4. Advantages/Disadvantages

Advantages:
- longer periods to accomplish lab-type activities
- only three classes to teach a day (unless you teach music - then four with band and chorus
- less students per semester to grade
- ninety minutes of planning time

Disadvantages:
- music classes that need to run all year long
- only having students for half a year - 1 semester
- classes can get overloaded

• need more classes (electives) in the schedule, because the students can take more throughout their high school career
• more staff needed
• when students miss a 90 minute class it's like missing two
• less teacher-to-teacher contact, more teacher-to-student contact (more teaching time usually involved)
• 90 minute study halls

5. Specific Suggestions:

Number 1 - Get on the planning committee and be an active member.
• Be vocal and don't let your program become unimportant.
• Try to come up with some sample schedules on your own (time frames).
• Let your parents help you with support and backing your program.

6. Additional Information:

I had much trouble at first convincing people that students would not be able to take band (for two credits) all year long, and the same for chorus. Also, it would not work for students if they wanted to be in both groups. Once I said that my two performing groups must meet be all year, we really started to research the possibilities. Yes, there are some disadvantages, but so far things are ok, and I am still searching out the perfect schedule.

Name: Erik E. Pointer
Position: Director of Instrumental Music
School: Richmond R-XVI Schools
              Richmond, Missouri

1. School Description:

The Richmond R-XVI High School is located in Richmond, MO., (population approximately 6000) and is a 3A school with a student population of approximately 600. Situated in the Missouri River Valley in Ray County, Richmond is approximately 40 miles northeast of Kansas City, MO.

2. Schedule Description:

We are currently using two different systems; an eight block schedule at the high school level (90 minute periods) and a ten block schedule (75 minutes) at the middle school level. These are simply divided into Red and White Days, no activity period is regularly scheduled.

3. Development of Current Schedule:

I started the process around 1992, studying ramifications of the schedule, dealing with shuffling of my class schedule (I have the entire program myself), rehearsal and performance problems, the writing of new classes, and curriculum concerns. The district was planning to go online with the block schedule 1994-95, but delayed it a year. From the time of the inception of the idea of the block in 1992, I did as many studies of different schedules as possible to see what would benefit the students most, and still not compromise the music making that was taking place in the entire program. I also did much reading, looking at other programs (mostly their problems), and spending time figuring out the good things about the block, and how to utilize them without completely revamping something that was not broken. Through the use of studies and proof of success, I convinced my middle school principal that my beginning band was on the same level as a reading class at the elementary level, and the students needed daily reinforcement of many basic language and motor skills (among others). Although the school year, 1996-97 is the opening year of the ten block system at Richmond Middle School (one year later than the eight block system at Richmond High School), the beginning program does not seem to be suffering. It is too early to tell about the Seventh Grade Band and the Eighth Grade Band which meet on alternate red and white days. Next school year we are slated to hire an associate band person to share the load at both schools (using a type of vertical instructional staffing), and also expand the extra course offerings in the music area to include an instrumental performance skills class, a music appreciation laboratory, and a computer music class. All but the computer music class is already being offered at the high school level. At the high school level we have historically (for the last 30 years) held some extra rehearsals and sectional rehearsals before the school day begins. During concert band, we usually have one brass sectional, one percussion sectional, one woodwind sectional, and one full ensemble rehearsal, each at 7:00 a.m., to prepare for different performances. The students and parents are very cooperative in this effort, and when using these sectional rehearsals in a way that enhances the red-white scheduling, the system seems to work. Although our district, like most others, did the standard in-service routes for the professional staff (vanilla at best), and the informational meetings for parents, the lion's share of the studies to keep the instrumental program intact, growing, and viable, was self-employed.

4. Advantages/Disadvantages

Besides all the obvious disadvantages to the way we have all been used to working in the profession through the years, the biggest concerns I have are:

a.) More limited contact with students from a personal standpoint, sometimes doesn't help the personal (not just musical) development of the student (see Mr. Holland's Opus).
b.) Although the students don't always realize it, they have as much adjustment to make to the system as we do, and sometimes their feeling of urgency in any given project, musical or otherwise, can be slightly *ritardando.*

NOTE: I really enjoy being able to use different teaching and rehearsal strategies that I rarely had time for, before the advent of the block system. Doing music historical work, listening to recordings, musical discussions, and student self-adjudications, definitely add to the retention of the material and add to the understanding and performance level of the students (I have employed all of these in my rehearsals for years, but now they really can make a difference because of the time element allowing for closure of each activity).

5. Specific Suggestions:

Do your homework, look at all the possibilities, and use your energies to find a way to make it work in your circumstance. Remember that some years ago, the one-room school house, without instrumental music, was considered to be the only way to educate children. The people advocating that system never thought that a multi-period school day with an expanded curriculum would ever work. We need to find a way to <u>evolve</u>, not <u>dissolve</u>, our programs in a way that benefits the entire student focus. I only hope administrators and teachers alike continue to not do what is best or easiest for them, what is best for the building, what is best for the parents, what is best for the schedule, what is best for the staff, or what is best for the budget. WE SHOULD ONLY DO WHAT IS BEST FOR THE STUDENTS AND THEIR QUEST FOR KNOWLEDGE OF ANY KIND.

Name: Marsha Borovicea
Position: Director of Choral Activities
School: Chaparral High School
           Las Vegas, Nevada

1. School Description:

• Chapparal High School is located in the southeast area of Las Vegas
• 2600 students
• middle to lower middle class economic income level

2. Schedule Description:

• 3 periods (105 minutes each), every other day

3. Development of Current Schedule:

• 12 months of research and assessment of other block schedules

- administration, faculty, and parent representatives were involved in the decision
- in-service was held prior to school vote (67%+) to indoctrinate teachers
- subsequent training sessions have been held to assess success and evaluate for possible modifications

4. Advantages/Disadvantages:

- It's wonderful! - allowing for in-depth rehearsal procedures
- the musicianship of my singers has monumentally increased because I have more time to develop concepts and applications

5. Specific Suggestions:

- organize, organize, organize!!
- I've had to become far more organized in my planning and advance preparation for rehearsals.

6. Additional Information:

- only positive results!!
- my numbers are up (enrollment)
- my students' musicianship is better (more sensitive and interpretive)
- students are assuming more responsibility for their overall education

Name: Donna McCommon
Position: Choral Director
School: Pearl High School
          Pearl, Mississippi

1. School Description:

Pearl High School has an enrollment of 1050. The city of Pearl is in the Jackson Metro Area. Most of its residents are blue collar workers, although there seems to be a growth in the white collar population.

2. Schedule Description:

Monday - 1-7 periods, regular school day as follows:

8:25-9:21 - first period
9:25-10:20 - second period
10:24-11:19 - third period
11:23-12:42 - fourth period
12:46-1:40 - fifth period
1:44-2:38 - sixth period
2:42-3:35 - seventh period

Tuesday and Thursday - 1, 3, 5, 7 periods
Wednesday and Friday - 2,4, 6, 7 periods as follows:

8:25-10:20 - first/second period
10:24-12:42 - third/fourth period
12:46-2:38 - fifth/sixth period
2:42-3:35 - seventh period

3. Development of Current Schedule:

The principal we had at the time the change was made took the idea before the school board, and after investigating the reasons for suggesting the change, the school board voted to approve it. My schedule was kept basically the same with classes meeting the same class periods. There was an adjustment having two-hour rehearsals as compared to 55 minutes. I was originally against the schedule but now I love it. I do not see my students every day, but we seem to accomplish so much in the long rehearsals. We do take a break.

4. Advantages/Disadvantages:

Advantages:
• The longer rehearsal allows us to do more sectional rehearsal (I do have an assistant for part of the day), and gives a feeling of accomplishment because of longer time in rehearsal.

Disadvantages:
• not getting to see the students every day before a performance

5. Specific Suggestions:

Make sure that you adjust your rehearsal time so that you do not keep the students on one thing longer than necessary. Remember that their attention span will die if a good variety of time is not used.

6. Additional Information:

Our schedule did not change the classes into modules of 6 or 9 weeks. We just do not meet every class every day. Classes with labs now have time to do better work. Over all this schedule has worked for us.

Name: Kay Reat
Position: Assistant Principal for Instruction
Name: Kathryn Zetterstrom
Position: Choir Director
Name: Larry Garrett
Position: Orchestra Director
School: Monterey High School
              Lubbock, Texas

1. School Description:

• 41 year old urban school
• 1620 students, grades 10-12
• changing demographics from 8% minority population
to 35% minority population in 8 years

2. Schedule Description:

• A/B block schedule: 90-minute classes which meet on
alternating days

3. Development of Current Schedule:

Monterey High School began research into block
scheduling with a visit to North Garland High School in
Texas in late September, 1993.   Six additional Texas
high schools were visited.   Schedule changes for the
1994-95 school year were discussed at a late October,
1993 site based decision council meeting.   Discussion
continued throughout the fall, and the site-based
council presented a proposed block schedule for 1994-
95 to the PTA in early January, 1995.   A daily schedule
containing modifications   suggested by parents,
teachers, and others was presented at a mid-February
meeting.

4. Advantages/Disadvantages:

Choir:
The biggest advantage of block scheduling I have experienced is that, since I'm "double-blocked", I can rehearse my choirs 90 minutes **every** day.
The major disadvantage for **me**, lies within the advantage, and that is that so many students can not be a part of my program **because** I'm double-blocked. And if I single-block my classes, I'll have a new set of problems because I'll only rehearse every **other** day.

Orchestra:
Advantages:
• 90 minutes rehearsal each day, gives time to devote to technique, warm-up, and detailed rehearsal
Disadvantages:
• hard to avoid schedule conflicts with a portion of your members
• don't get to see everyone every day, can cause continuity problems - announcements, details

5. Specific Suggestions:

Choir:
When deciding whether or not any of your classes will be double-blocked, make sure your student base can support it. If classes are only single-blocked, design a rehearsal schedule that makes the most out of your 90 minutes since you will only see your students every other day.

Orchestra:
Make announcements consistently over several days to "catch" all students. Written announcements can also be used. Tutor students who have class every other day to move them along.

6. Additional Information:

Choir:
Block scheduling, in my opinion, is most helpful and advantageous if you can support a double-blocked class where you see your students every day. That certainly allows for maximum rehearsal time and continuity.

Name: David F. Cree
Position: High School Band Director
School: Bellefonte Area High School
             Bellefonte, Pennsylvania

1. School Description:

The Bellefonte Area School District is an urban/rural school district in the center of Pennsylvania, about 10 miles from Penn State University. We have about 2700 students K-12.

2. Schedule Description:

We are utilizing a "modified block" schedule. Three days per week we have 8 periods with 42 minute each. Two days per week we have 4 period days with each period lasting approximately 90 minutes each.

3. Development of Current Schedule:

Five or six years ago the district began the process by forming a committee with the purpose of investigating different schedules. The committee involved both teachers and administrators. We met monthly for nearly a year, and then instituted the system on a "trial basis. We have continued to refine the schedule through input from staff, parents, and administrators.

4. Advantages/Disadvantages:

Advantages would include providing the opportunity for extended lessons, science labs, and projects, during the 90-minute periods. Disadvantages have included an impact on rehearsal time for performance classes, as well as making scheduling difficult for Fine Arts students to take AP classes.

5. Specific Suggestions:

This is not a bad compromise for those schools headed towards block scheduling or intensive scheduling. We have not lost Fine Arts class offerings, but probably have lost a bit in numbers and student contact time.

6. Additional Information:

PMEA NEWS, our state music educators journal, devoted an entire issue to the subject of Block Scheduling. I would recommend writing to Dr. Richard Merrell, editor of PMEA NEWS, at 823 Old Westtown Road, West Chester, PA 19382-5276 for a copy of the May, 1996 issue.

Name: Tony Martinez
Position: Instrumental Music Supervisor
School: Western Heights High School
               Oklahoma City, Oklahoma

1. School Description:

- 750 students, 9-12
- suburb just outside of southwestern Oklahoma City

2. Schedule Description:

- straight block
- solids last 1 semester
- band meets every day all year

3. Development of Current Schedule:

- a lot of meetings with principals and superintendents
- took a year to develop
- going with the choir director and presenting a united front helped
- Fine Arts is the largest extra curricular here

4. Advantages/Disadvantages:

Advantages:
- more time with students
Disadvantages:
- limits number of classes in schedule

5. Specific Suggestions:

- get in and be active in the early planning stages
- when there are proposals on the table, track your students through the 4 years to see if they work

Name: William Naydan
Position: Choral Director
School: Hatboro-Horsham High School
                  Horsham, Pennsylvania

1. School Description:

- 9-12 high school of 1300 students
- 25 miles north of Philadelphia
- middle to upper middle class suburb

2. Schedule Description:

- 4x4 block, 83 minutes per period

3. Development of Current Schedule:

- 2 years of study and implementation with each department's input
- parent and student orientation
- much teacher in-service
- annual assessments of effectiveness by faculty, students, and parents

4. Advantages/Disadvantages:

Advantages:
- more time on task

Disadvantages:
- difficult to see all students at once for rehearsals

5. Specific Suggestions:

- try a 6-day rotation with music meeting every other day

Name: Jim Howell
Position: Instrumental Music Teacher
School: La Grande High School
              La Grande, Oregon

1. School Description:

• 930 students, 9-12
• town of 12,000 in relatively isolated northeast Oregon area
• music program is supported by the community, and by the administration

2. Schedule Description:

• 4 - 88 minute blocks/day
• All meet daily except music and a few select other alternating-day required classes. Classes change at the semester. Music students may transfer in or out at that time, but most are in by choice for the year. Music meets everyday (1 semester = 1/2 credit).

3. Development of Current Schedule:

Our schedule was one of the first blocks in Oregon and was teacher-initiated and generated over a 1 1/2 year period with 1/2 day per month of staff development time, partially funded with private grant money. We had to persuade the school board to allow us to try our ideas. We could have done better at preparing parents for what was going to happen. We survived this well, but had to counter many misunderstandings for lack of preventative "PR". Our building principal was supportive all along and supported teacher-driven innovation. We took much "flak" from higher up.

4. Advantages/Disadvantages:

Eighty-eight minute rehearsals are profoundly more productive compared to two 48 minute ones. Kids adapted well to writing assignments down and working on them on days we did not meet (director also). Initially we had inadequate alternating-day classes to accommodate music students on non-music days. That has/is improving.

5. Specific Suggestions:

Try to institute a block as an A-day, B-day, 8 classes per semester if possible. This appears to me to have a beneficial effect on music programs. If you are using a 4-period day, semester long classes are the only option. Insist on alternating day classes, including REQUIRED classes opposite music. Those teachers will soon enjoy that batch of kids
too ...

6. Additional Information:

We have made lunch 1 hour. One half of that for teachers is access time in our rooms for kids needing help/makeup. Every other Wednesday begins with an 80-minute block of time not required for students except those seeking help or making up tests/assignments/labs from excused absences. This is necessary because students miss so much in one 88 minute block when they are gone.

For some of these teachers, the "process" of developing a block scheduling system for their individual schools involved cooperative planning with input from many sources and on-going assessment. For other teachers, the process was somewhat "dictated". And in at least one case, the block scheduling efforts were teacher-driven. Some teachers reported "good" things happening to their music programs. Others mentioned new "challenges" brought on by a new scheduling system. All of the music teachers seemed involved and determined to "make it work" individually, one program at a time.

CHAPTER 5

Suggestions for Becoming Involved, Informed, And Building Networks for Sharing Information

Most all music educators who indicated that they were having success with block scheduling suggested two important issues: 1) becoming adequately informed about block scheduling and the options which should be considered, and 2) becoming involved in the planning, decision, and scheduling process. Jo and Bruce Caldwell along with other leaders of the Washington Music Educators Association (WMEA) shared the following advice for music educators having to consider moving to block scheduling. This feature article on Block Scheduling appeared in the March 1996 issue of the WMEA *Voice*. The following is presented with permission.

Most importantly, you must believe passionately that music education does, indeed, matter.

1. It is absolutely critical that music teachers get in on the ground floor when these ideas originate. Get on the scheduling committee.

2. Build coalitions with other curriculum areas that

will be concerned about not having students all year long: math, foreign language, business, yearbook, newspaper, and drama.

3.   Establish early and frequent communication with your staff, including administrators.

4.   Make sure parents are informed and involved in the process. Communicate regularly with them. Educate your audiences.

5.   Have facts. Be specific when you talk to people. Educate everyone about why music is valuable to kids' education. Parents are interested in what students learn. Relate what arts education does for students. Some excellent sources of information include: *Phi Delta Kappan*, January 1994; *Teaching Music*, December 1994, April 1995, and December 1995; *Voice*, January 1996; and MENC Information Services, 1-800-336-3768.

6.   Know about different types of schedules and what they do. Don't just settle for a generic schedule, see exactly what that schedule will look like in your school, with your staff. Changes are coming. Be willing to compromise. Don't be narrowly focused; work to find a schedule that will accommodate everybody's needs.

7. Be a team player. Be a part of everything. It is the only way you can protect your program.

8. Let people know that you carry a big load; your big load saves them money.

9. Become familiar with information from MENC and network with others who have interest in and experience with the problems you are facing. There is an extensive bibliography of textbooks and journals, published in 1994 by the American Bandmasters Association, *Strategic Planning for Instrumental Education*. Individual studies have been done: High School Restructuring (*Alternate Use of School Time*), *Block Scheduling: Implications for Music Educators*, prepared for the Kentucky Coalition for Music Education, February 1995; *The Effects of the Four Period Day on Colorado High School Performing Arts Classes* by Gary Hall, June 1992, Masters Thesis, Dave Baldock, Cashmere, 1995.

10. Don't assume anything. The bottom line is often the building administrator who thinks the public wants change and sees block scheduling as a quick, visible change. Keep in mind that many on your staff will have heard that the longer periods mean less stress for teachers, making their jobs seem easier. Keep the

focus on what is best for kids' education.

Important Factors for Music in a Schedule

Jo and Bruce Caldwell also suggest that "there are several factors that music teachers should lobby for if a schedule change is imminent. If these concepts can be met, the music program has a reasonable chance for survival, or perhaps even success."

1. **An administration that actively supports music education.** Nothing is more important than an administration who will work to see that there is a variety of good music classes available on a user-friendly schedule, and that students can take music classes.

2. **Year-long classes.** Whether daily or alternating, the ability of students to take music all year makes a big difference in the students staying with the class. It is difficult to keep students in the program when a full credit is given for a semester's work.

3. **Freedom from scheduling conflicts.** Music students (frequently the best academic students in the school) often have only one choice for their music class. If that choice is up against a singleton requirement (for

graduation or college entrance), or integrated classes (often called blocked or tracked - sometimes double periods) then music students are forced out, usually never to return.

4. **Reasonable options for music students.** If a split block is offered, are there reasonable classes the music student can take with split? (Or is it just a different music class or a very limited choice of classes that students do not want to take all of their high school years?) "Offerings" must align with "reality" or else it's just rhetorical condescension that music students are considered in schedule building.

5. **Graduation waivers and credit options.** If schedules are providing conflicts or credit limits, then administrators must be willing to grant waivers to music students when needed to provide continuity for those students.

6. **Teacher training.** Simply repeating what was said before, music teachers need unique training and different assistance than other teachers. Music is already an outcome-based curriculum.

Creative Ways to Help
Music Succeed in a Block Schedule

The following 17 suggestions are most important to keep in mind when looking for ideas and options in dealing with block scheduling. These suggestions are from a presentation to the Wisconsin Music Educators Association entitled - *Block Scheduling and The Performance Based Music Program*. These responses are a result of an investigation into block scheduling by Kevin Meidl, Director of Choral Music Studies, at Appleton West High School in Appleton, Wisconsin. These creative ways include input from music educators from 32 schools in 13 states across the country and are presented with permission.

"Following are some elements within block scheduled schools which tend to support performance based music programs. It is important to keep in mind that what works for one school might not work in the next, or might need modification."

1. Increase graduation requirements with a requirement that all students take four credits or blocks per semester, and not less than 30 credits over four years.

2. Require students not to take more than one credit

in any particular discipline during any school year, with the exception of performance music classes, and other students who have fulfilled all graduation requirements (likely only second semester juniors and seniors).

3. Deny students the opportunity to take their senior English class early, or other classes generally taken during the fourth year of high school.

4. If working with a rotating A/B block, schedule "Varsity Level" performing groups during the same block in order to share students. Lots of creative opportunities are presented by this process and enrollment in all programs can increase (but particularly in the choir).

5. If working with a rotating A/B block, schedule AP classes or Honors classes in rotation with "Varsity Level" performing ensembles.

6. If working with either an A/B system or a Straight 4x4 block, use the 3rd period block for OVERLAPPING choirs, bands, and orchestra. In many models this block will contain at least an additional 20 minutes for lunch. This would allow for a mixed choir in the middle of two unisex choirs. It might also allow for instrumental sectionals with full band in the middle.

7. If working with a straight block, have the upper level performing groups meet every day for two credits (one full block all year) while the younger students come every other day rotating with Physical Education or another required class.

8. Offer more elective one-credit, one-semester ensembles. A second semester Jazz Band, Madrigal Choir, Chamber Orchestra, or even a larger performing ensemble could find many students looking for a one semester elective. Audition them in the spring and plug them into the ensemble you would like to offer. In addition, non-performance music classes offered for one credit will be in high demand (i.e., theory, history, appreciation, or the study of a particular speciality area).

9. Offer during the school day, for one semester and one credit, the spring musical, or the fall musical, or touring choir rehearsal or even marching band. In addition to your regular band or choir rehearsal, this one credit, ninety minute class could produce some exciting results and take away many of the evening rehearsals.

10. Convince the teachers and administrators in your school that a pull-out lesson program is necessary if

you go to a block system. One school mandated that a pull-out would happen only from English classes and once each month for thirty minutes (it was a small school!).

11. Propose a "Teamed Block" where an entire year will be spent studying specific types of music, the world events surrounding the creation of the art, other related art of the period, historical points of interest, etc. Team yourself with an art teacher, a history teacher, a humanities teacher, and English or literature teachers, etc. and together design a structure which will involve all of the ensemble students and teachers working toward the same interrelated, interdisciplinary lecture concerts, art shows, tours and other types of final projects. (If you planned to travel with your orchestra to Italy and Greece next summer, it would make a wonderful year of study and preparation).

12. Get a school board commitment to add fine arts staff. To move to a block with demands students take two credits instead of one, it would also mean that the music teacher would teach two credits instead of one. This is a doubling of contact time. While other teachers around the school may be decreasing their semester load by half, the music teacher maybe increasing by 100% the amount of time in front of the band. Those

students must now count as two instead of one. Help is needed to continue to offer the same program currently in the traditional schedule. If a second or third is added, there are many possibilities for team teaching, rotating activities, and shared ensembles.

13. In some cases, the modification of a Straight Block with "Skinnies" (*singleton classes*) can assist scheduling. Find a department or teacher to teach the other half of the block. This person or department needs to be strongly interested in teaching an all-year one credit class opposite your performing ensemble. It should also be an offering which students would need to have anyway (i.e., keyboarding, a basic math class, speech, or study skills).

14. The school scheduler (usually an assistant principal in charge of curriculum) must become your new best friend. This person needs to be as open-minded, and creative as possible to facilitate the special needs of the performance music program. Students should not be making unusual choices in order to be in a performing ensemble. Further, the scheduler must keep in mind the music classes as he/she builds the rest of the schedule. In a traditional schedule, music classes tend to be scheduled first because of their size and the strong appeal for large numbers of motivated students.

This should remain the same under a block schedule. At that point as well, rules should be entered into the scheduling program which permit only music students to have two credits of this one discipline during the same school year (many other rules should be added as well about how long a student can be away from a foreign language, math, or other curricular sequence of classes).

15. The guidance counselors must become your next closest friends. They have to SELL, along with you to parents and students, that there is no problem taking two credits of a music class (or 25% of their high school schedule). They need to really believe it . . . or numbers are likely to go down. As hard as you work on the students in your class to believe they can take music all year, you must work with the counselors to understand and communicate the same information. No matter how hard you work, it will come down to the fifteen minutes in the middle of the year when your student sits down one-to-one with that guidance counselor. You need to know that he/she is supportive.

16. The entire administrative team must be supportive of music's special needs under a block system. Your principal, and other administrators are absolutely key to the success of double-blocking in music. They need

to understand that there might not be a marching band for homecoming, or that there might not be a choir to sing at the school board function in the spring, if students are not allowed to FREELY elect two credits of a performing ensemble.

17. Be careful to be a problem solver, and not just an obstacle for the block scheduling committee to overcome. Parent groups can be helpful, but don't enlist the army unless you have thought well about the consequences. It is easy with this issue to appear self-serving and not open to other educational needs of the student. If you believe block scheduling will ruin your music program, then use the tools listed above to address issues. Even as you fight to keep the traditional schedule, work hard (and quietly) to create the best possible situation for your program if your school does adopt block scheduling.

CHAPTER 6

Block Scheduling and School Music Programs
- Some Closing Thoughts -

"The jury is still out" is an appropriate closing statement at this time for the impact of block scheduling on school music programs. We have found some teachers who love block scheduling, some who hate block scheduling, some who are unsure about block scheduling, and some whose feelings about block scheduling change almost daily. We have found no "typical" or "model" high school schedule in any of the states that we have studied. Perhaps not surprisingly, one schedule "does not fit all." It seems important to note, however, that if America's schools are to be reinvented around learning and not time, careful attention must be given to data that indicate **any** decline in **any academic area** within a school due to scheduling conflicts. It is difficult for teachers to teach and for students to learn if students are not present.

Block scheduling seems to be "working" for music programs where teachers and administrators work together to individualize a schedule within the context of **their total school**. Because block scheduling is a relatively "new" idea for many schools, ongoing, long-term study is needed to monitor the effects of block scheduling on school music programs. **Time may be an important factor**.

David Elliot, in **Music Matters** (1995), states that "the future of music education - and, perhaps, the future of education itself - lies in facing our problems as challenges..." Block scheduling offers many challenges. However, we must accept the challenges, because as caring music education professionals, we know individually and collectively, that **music education does, indeed, matter**.

CHAPTER 7

Where to Look for Help -
Selected References

General - Block Scheduling

Boarman, Gerald R. and Barbara S. Kirkpatrick. "The Hybrid Schedule: Scheduling to the Curriculum." *NASSP Bulletin,* May 1995, 79: 42-52.

Brandt, Ron. "On Restructuring Schools: A Conversation with Fred Newman." *Educational Leadership.* November 1995, 53/3: 70-73.

Buckman, Daniel C. and Bonnie Besten King, and Shelia Ryan. "Block Scheduling: A Means to Improve School Climate." *NASSP Bulletin,* May 1995, 79: 9-18.

Canady, Robert Lynn. *Elementary Parallel Block Scheduling.* The Video Journal of Education. Salt Lake City, 1994. Videocassette.

Canady, Robert Lynn. Presenter. *High School Block Scheduling.* TheVideo Journal of Education. Salt Lake City, 1994. Videocassette.

Canady, Robert Lynn, and Michael D. Rettig. *Block Scheduling: A Catalyst for Change in High Schools.* Princeton: Eye on Education, 1995.

Canady, Robert Lynn, and Michael D. Rettig. "The Power of Innovative Scheduling." *Educational Leadership.* November 1995, 53/3: 4-10..

Canady, Robert Lynn, and Michael D. Rettig. "Unlocking the Lockstep High School Schedule." *Phi Delta Kappan,* December 1993, 75: 310-314.

Carroll, Joseph M. "The Copernican Plan Evaluated: The Evolution of a Revolution." *Phi Delta Kappan,* October 1994, 76: 104-110, 112-113.

Carroll, Joseph M. "The Copernican Plan: Restructuring the American High School." *Phi Delta Kappan,* January 1990, 71: 358-365.

Carroll, Joseph M. *The Copernican Plan: Restructuring the American High School.* Topsfield, MA: Copernican Associates, 1989.

Cawelti, Gordon. *High School Restructuring: A National Study.* Arlington: Educational Research Service Report, 1994.

Edwards, Clarence M. Jr. "The 4x4 Plan." *Educational Leadership*, November 1995, 53/3: 16-19.

Edwards, Clarence M. Jr. "Virginia's 4x4 High Schools: High School, College, and More." *NASSP Bulletin*, May 1995, 79: 23-41.

Hackman, Donald G. "Ten Guidelines for Implementing Block Scheduling." *Educational Leadership,* November 1995, 53/3: 24-27.

Huff, A. Leroy. "Flexible Block Scheduling: It Works for Us." *NASSP Bulletin*, May 1995, 79: 19-22.

Kruse, Carol A. and Gary D. Kruse. "The Master Schedule and Learning: Improving the Quality of Education." *NASSP Bulletin,* May 1995, 79: 1-8.

Music Educators National Conference. "Critical Issues in Education Reform Affecting Music and the Arts. Selected Bibliography." Reston: Music Educators National Conference, 1995.

National Commission on Excellence in Education. *A Nation at Risk*. Cambridge, MA: USA Research, 1984.

National Center for Education Statistics. *Digest of Education Statistics*. Washington, D.C.: Office of Educational Research and Improvement - U.S. Government Printing Office, 1993.

National Education Commission on Time and Learning. *Prisoners of Time*. Washington, D.C.: U.S. Government Printing Office, 1994

O'Neil, John. "Finding Time to Learn." *Educational Leadership,* November 1995, 53/6: 11-15..

Rettig, Michael D. *Directory of High School Scheduling Models in Virginia: 1995-96 School Year*. Harrisonburg, VA: James Madison University, 1996.

Shortt, Thomas L., and Yvonne Thayer. "What Can We Expect to See in the Next Generation of Block Scheduling?" *NASSP Bulletin,* May 1995, 79: 53-62.

Sizer, Theodore. *Horace's Compromise: The Dilemma of the American High School*. Boston: Houghton Mifflin, 1992.

Wilson, Cheryl. "The 4x4 Block System: A Workable Alternative." *NASSP Bulletin,* May 1995, 79: 63-65.

Music - Block Scheduling

Blocher, Larry, and Richard Miles. "An Analysis of Block Scheduling on High School Music Programs." Report presented at the "Critical Issues in Music Teacher Education Symposium," Univeristy of Colorado-Boulder, October 1996.

Blocher, Larry, and Richard Miles. "Block Scheduling." Michigan School Band and Orchestra Association *Spring Journal*, Volume 56/2, 1996: 57-60.

Blocher, Larry, and Richard Miles. "Block Scheduling and Public School Music Programs - A View from the Inside Out." A Report presented at the Summer Music Symposium, Kansas State University, June 1996 and the Kansas Bandmasters Association Convention, June 1996.

Blocher, Larry, and Richard Miles. "Block Scheduling - Making a Research Connection." *Kansas Music Review*, Volume 58/4, November 1996.

Blocher, Larry, and Richard Miles. *High School Restructuring - Block Scheduling: Implications for Music Educators.* Louisville: Kentucky Coalition for Music Education, 1995.

Blocher, Larry, and Richard Miles. "A Survey of Block Scheduling Implementation in Secondary Music Programs in Indiana." Report prepared for the Indiana Department of Education, 1995.

Blocher, Larry, and Richard Miles. "A Survey of Block Scheduling Implementation in Secondary Music Programs in Kentucky." Report prepared for the Kentucky Music Educators Association, 1995.

Blocher, Larry, and Richard Miles. "A Survey of Block Scheduling Implementation in Secondary Music Programs in Michigan." Report prepared for the Michigan School Band and Orchestra Association, 1996.

Blocher, Larry, and Richard Miles. "A Survey of Block Scheduling Implementation in Secondary Music Programs in Wisconsin." Report prepared for the Wisconsin Music Educators Association, 1996.

Blocher, Larry, and Richard Miles (contributors). *High School Restructuring: Additional Resources.* Louisville: Kentucky Coalition for Music Education, 1996.

Benham, John and Stephen Benham. "The Perils of Block Scheduling: This Latest Folly is Worse Than the New Math." *The Instrumentalist,* August 1996, 51/1: 30-32.

Bradley, Lynne. "Educational Reform and Restructuring: Defining our Terms." *Choral Journal,* November 1995, 36/4: 25-29.

Cutietta, Robert, Donald L. Hamann, and Linda Miller Walker. *Spin-Offs - The Extra-Musical Advantages of a Musical Education*. Elkhart: United Musical Instruments U.S.A., Inc., 1995.

Hall, Gary E. "The Effects of the Four Period Day on Colorado High School Performing Arts Classes." A Descriptive Study Presented to the Faculty of the Division of Graduate Studies, Adams State College, Alamosa, Colorado, 1992.

Harding, Robert A. "Prepare to Fight for Your Music Program." *Music Educators Journal*, January 1992, 78: 5, 20, 22-23.

Hinckley, June, ed. *Music at the Middle Level: Building Strong Programs*. Reston: Music Educators National Conference, 1994.

Hook, Martin. "Block Scheduling and Its Effect on Secondary-School Music Performance Classes." *Choral Journal*, November 1995, 36/4: 27-29.

Hoffman, Elizabeth. "A Closer Look at Block Scheduling." *Teaching Music*, April 1995, 2/5: 42-43.

Lehman, Paul R. "Priorities and Pitfalls of Music Education: An Open Letter." *NASSP Bulletin*, March 1988, 72: 98-104.

Meidl, Kevin. "Block Scheduling and the Performance Based Music Program." Report prepared for the Wisconsin Music Educators Association, March 1995.

Milleman, Jon. "4x4 Scheduling and the Angola High School Band." *BD Guide*, May/June 1996, 10/5: 28-31.

Miller, Allan, and Dorita Coen. "The Case for Music in the Schools." *Phi Delta Kappan,* Februaary 1994, 75/6.

Music Educators National Conference. *"An Agenda for Excellence in Music at the Middle-Level: A Statement by MENC on Middle Level Music Education."* Reston: Music Educators National Conference, 1994.

Music Educators National Conference. *Scheduling Time for Music.* Reston: Music Educators National Conference, 1995.

Oddleifson, Eric. "What Do We Want Our Schools to Do? The Arts Taught During the School Day as Serious Subjects Produce Young People Who Are Indeed 'Educated'." *Phi Delta Kappan*, February 1994, 75/6.

Schuler, Scott C. "Why High School Students Should Study the Arts." *Music Educators Journal*, July 1996, 83/1: 22-26.

Warrener, John J. "Floating Schedule for a Sinking Budget." *Music Educators Journal,* May 1984, 70: 54-57.

Wisconsin Music Educators Association. *Block Scheduling and the Music Program.* Produced and directed by the Wisconsin Music Educators Association. 66 min. 13 sec. Professional Development Series, 1995. Videocassette.

Year-Round Schools

Anderson, Julia. "Alternative Approaches to Organizing the School Day and Year." *School Administrator*, March 1994, 51: 3, 8-11, 15.

Chen, Zengshu. "Year-Round Education: High School Student Achievement and Teacher/ Administrator Attitudes." Ph.D. diss., United States International University, 1994.

Day, Susan H. "Teaching Orchestra on a Year-Round Schedule." *Teaching Music*, August 1996, 83/1: 33-35.

Hawkins, Sandy. *From Parent to Parent: A Look at Year-Round Education.* San Diego: National Association for Year-Round Education, 1992.

Natale, Jo Anna. "Success Stories in Year-Round Schooling." *American School Board Journal*, July 1992, 178: 29.

Trimis, Edward. "Can Year-Round Scheduling Work for Your Program?" *Music Educators Journal*, September 1990, 77: 50-52.

Weaver, Tyler. *Year-Round Education.* ERIC Clearinghouse on Educational Management, Office of Educational Research and Improvement, 1992.

White, William D. "Year-Round No More." *American School Board Journal*, July 1992, 178: 7, 27-28, 30.

ABOUT THE AUTHORS

Dr. Larry R. Blocher, is Associate Professor of Music Education, Associate Director of Bands, and Director of Music Education at Wichita State University in Wichita, Kansas. Dr. Blocher received his BME and MM (music education and performance) degrees from Morehead State University in Kentucky, and his Ph.D. in Music Education from The Florida State University. Dr. Blocher is active as a guest clinician/conductor and has presented clinic/research sessions at international, national, regional, and state conferences in the area of instrumental music teacher preparation.

Dr. Richard B. Miles, Director of Bands at Morehead State University in Kentucky, holds a Doctor of Philosophy degree from The Florida State University and undergraduate and graduate degrees from Appalachian State University and the University of Illinois. Since coming to MSU in 1985, the MSU Symphony Band has been selected to perform for conventions of the Music Educators National Conference, College Band Directors National Association, National Band Association, and the Kentucky Music Educators Association. Dr. Miles has 23 years of teaching experience at the university and secondary school levels, and serves nationally and internationally as a guest conductor, consultant, and clinician.

Dr. Blocher and Dr. Miles are coauthors of *Teaching Music through Performance in Band* (GIA Publications, 1996), *High School Restructuring - Block Scheduling: Implications for Music Educators* (Kentucky Coalition for Music Education, 1995), and contributors to *High School Restructuring: Additional Resources* (Kentucky Coalition for Music Education, 1996).